Country Living
COUNTRY CHRISTMAS

Country Living

COUNTRY CHRISTMAS

BO NILES

with quotations from
Jo Northrop,
Simple Country Pleasures

HEARST BOOKS
New York

Library of Congress Catalog Card Number: 90-80313
ISBN: 0-688-09738-3

Printed in Singapore

First Edition

1 2 3 4 5 6 7 8 9 10

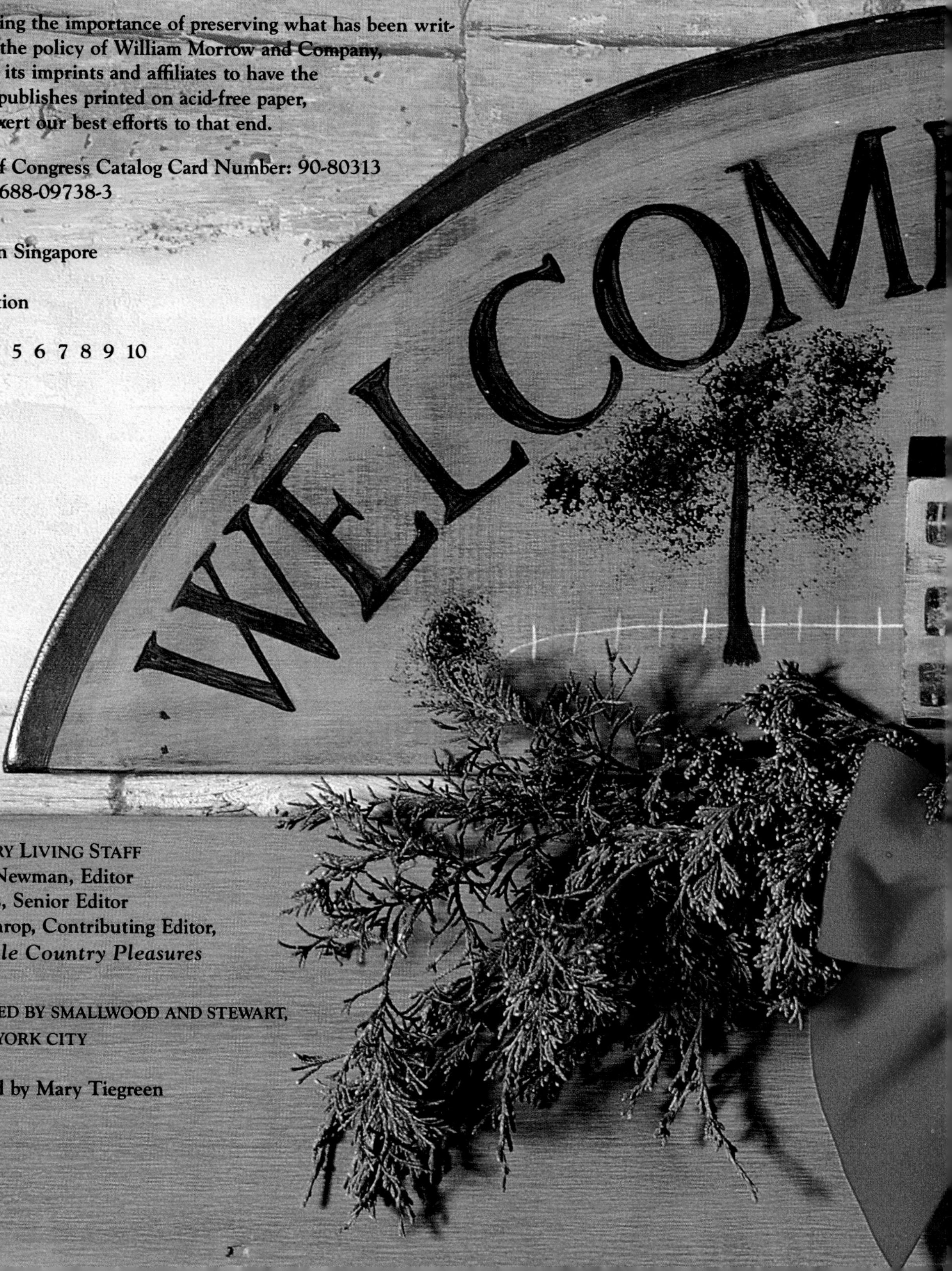

COUNTRY LIVING STAFF
Rachel Newman, Editor
Bo Niles, Senior Editor
Jo Northrop, Contributing Editor,
   Simple Country Pleasures

PRODUCED BY SMALLWOOD AND STEWART,
   NEW YORK CITY

Designed by Mary Tiegreen

CONTENTS

Foreword

very year, as the days grow shorter and colder, signaling the onset of the holiday season, we at *Country Living,* like you, prepare to celebrate America's favorite holiday: Christmas. And I thought: after our first decade of publication, how wonderful it would be to gather our favorite photographs of the rooms and trees and foods and ornaments—of everything we've loved best that has appeared in our pages over the years—and make a book that could extend the feeling of joy into the rest of the year! As we travel across the country to photograph our Christmas stories each year, we find that many of the wonderful people we meet prepare for this beloved holiday all year long, even if it simply entails gathering ideas and then filing them, perhaps, at the back of their minds to inspire them when the season approaches. Or, conversely, perhaps they may keep an eye out all year long, buying an antique tree decoration at a fair or a toy at an auction or a shop they love to visit, or they handcraft something special, or they clip a recipe and save it to

make up a personal and tasty treat to give to someone. Because, to them—and to us—Christmas is somehow always around the corner. It seems, indeed, as if the Christmas season is actually lengthening; we notice Santas smiling from shop windows as soon as the witches of Halloween have winged away on their broomsticks, and trees and decorations linger after the last bit of left-over turkey has been consumed—even after the last Champagne bubble of the New Year has fizzed off into resolutions for the future. I feel there is a need to sustain the warmth, the sharing, the joy; it is to this need that we speak in this book. We wanted to prolong Christmas, to enjoy its special warmth all year round. For the spirit of Christmas is a gift from heart and hearth and its magic and surprise, delight and love are values we always hold dear.

Rachel Newman
EDITOR
Country Living

Introduction

hristmas: The very word sings, sighs, whispers like a cold breeze through a frost-dusted pine tree or a kiss of snow against an icy window pane. Christmas has become, in America, a holiday of fusion amidst confusion, of harmony within discord, of music and prayer and good will and hope and laughter and gifts. Christmas is a holiday of saints and children, of families, of young and old; Christmas envelops everyone and ignores no one. The vitality of this holiday, at the winter solstice when night is longest and day is curtailed, is warm, cheerful, and inspiring.

Christmas in America is magical and transcends all faiths and all cultures, even as it embraces all faiths and all cultures. Although the spirituality of this holiday has traditionally centered on the Christ Child, and the secular on Father Christmas or Santa Claus, the real heart of Christmas is home and hearth for one and all of us

Americans, joined together to share in the blessing that is our freedom. And although the Christmas we are familiar with derives most especially from the cultures of Britain, Germany, and Holland, the unique assimilation of peoples that comprise America has forged a distinctly and distinctively American holiday, one that happily absorbs a bit of this and a bit of that into one grand, special, and wonderful celebration. When we set out cookies and milk for Santa Claus, we evoke "Sinterklass" by his Dutch name; when we trim a tree with ornaments we are following a German tradition of tree trimming; when we pass around a potent glogg we are sharing a typical Scandinavian recipe; when we raise our voices in the

"Halleluiah Chorus" we are simply adding our voices to thousands of British choristers; and when we light the way to our houses with lanterns, we are emulating a Mexican custom. This holiday reaches out to everyone; the spirit of this season ignites candle and soul; the spirit of the season makes us all kin.

The elements of the country Christmas are simple and, in the purest sense, uncluttered: a tree, some greens, ribbons, cards, a meal, gifts to share, light from a candle or fire or from smiling eyes, a song or carol or hymn or even an oratorio.

Christmas is, quite simply, a time to celebrate. During this season, reaching and radiating from the feelings of gratitude shared at Thanksgiving all the way up to the resolutions of the New Year, we celebrate human kindness and the indomitable human spirit. This all-encompassing feeling of celebration may embrace a crêche or a menorah, a yule log or even just one candy cane, but, in doing so, it enwraps us all in one serene yet humble wish: God Bless Us Every One.

In the pages that follow, we want to share with you the Christmases we have enjoyed at *Country Living* over the last decade. So many wonderful people opened their homes and their hearts to us; because Christmas comes year after year, we are glad to re-enter some of the homes we have loved best—and, in doing so, we say to you all: Have a Happy Holiday!, wherever you are. In our hearts, we are with you—always.

Bo Niles
SENIOR EDITOR
Country Living

CHAPTER ONE

THE TRADITIONS OF CHRISTMAS

CHRISTMAS IN A YOUNG AMERICA

CHRISTMAS IN A YOUNG AMERICA

In a room reminiscent of a country dry-goods store, opposite left, a mini-forest of evergreens stands in testimony to an all-American idea: to fill a room, floor to ceiling, with a fragrant evergreen. Going into the woods—or to the Christmas tree nursery—and cutting a tree, hoisting it upon shoulder or car top, and setting it up: this is a tradition native to America. The huge tree symbolized—and still does—the strength and virility of this energetic nation. Other elements in the room harken to the frontier, too: a sled, a horse, a church, a doll, portraying country transport, country worship, and above all, the durability of human kindness and love. And it's all backed up, of course, by the American flag.

It seems hard to believe that Christmas as we know it today in America has not persisted since the first colonists set foot upon our our shores. But, in fact, Christmas was banned by our stern Puritan ancestors, who, reacting strongly to anything that reminded them of "relics of Popery," expressed a transplanted antagonism based upon a centuries-old conflict between the Catholic and Protestant faiths, and later the high-Anglican and low-Protestant sects. Over eighty percent of the earliest settlers to this New World were indeed Protestants, most hailing from England or Germany, and so, for a time, the Puritan ethic prevailed. But many settlers, especially those who came somewhat later to live in the southern colonies, condoned a convivial celebration, one of merriment and cheer and good food and companionship, as an antidote to the almost unendurable winters they experienced in this rugged new nation. As the settlers pressed westward, establishing homesteads along the frontier, they carried their traditions—both European-born and American-bred—with them, creating, slowly but surely, a new and truly all-American holiday. At first the celebrations comprised little more than a better meal, a

In the 1849 Pioneer Museum in historic Fredericksburg, Texas, above, a handmade Santa with his sack of toys is sheltered in a cedar-framed cheese strainer. Branches of yaupon, a type of holly found in the South, and berries add color.

15

single, simple homemade gift for each member of the family, a remembered song or carol. But as America grew and prospered, so did this holiday—into the Christmas we know and cherish today.

The roots of our American Christmas are many and myriad, but because so many of the earliest settlers emigrated to this country from England, the most powerful influence upon the holiday derived from the British "Christes Maesse"—or Christ's Mass—a church-ordained re-enactment of the nativity. As early as the fourth century A.D. Christians adopted December 25th as Christ's birthdate, and had set aside Epiphany—the Twelfth Day of Christmas—for the arrival of the Wise Men, and for Christ's baptism. Early festivities also wove into the biblical tale aspects of pagan celebrations of the winter solstice and the week-long Roman Saturnalia, when gifts were traditionally passed out among children and the poor. Since the Middle Ages, the Yule log and ever-greens—symbolizing survival and eternal life—have been associated with this season, not only in England but in Eastern Europe and in Scandinavia as well. And although Christmas has its roots in a holy day, the secular aspects of the holiday have become just as important in England and in this country.

Secular celebrations occurred on different days; the holy day remained the 25th. Gift-giving and feasting transpired on St. Nicholas's Day on December 6th in Holland; the Epiphany on January 6th was reserved for gift-giving in Italy when the Befana, an old crone, came to place treats in children's shoes. Similarly, in France, presents were traditionally left in shoes set just beyond the door. When waves of immigration intensified during the nineteenth century, a resurgence of longing for tolerance and for the freedom of personal expression of faith prevailed—and the American holiday absorbed influences from many nations, both in specific rituals and in a general spirit of joy and good will as well.

From Germans, Americans adopted the practice of cutting and decorating a tree. In Germany, the tree typically was small and sat on a table, above, but in America, where trees grew in abundance, evergreens were room-size. Prince Albert, Queen Victoria's husband and a German, popularized the Christmas tree in England. The Germans called the fir the "Paradise Tree," commemorating the feast of Adam and Eve, and they hung it with wafers and lighted candles to symbolize Christ; later they perfected the manufacture of glass ornaments and gaily painted molded figures. After boycotts imposed on Germany following World War I, ornaments were produced in quantity in the United States.

Tapestry ribbon and pheasant feathers impart an elegant touch to an enormous wreath hanging in an English-style library, above. Many of the most beloved Christmas traditions such as caroling, sending Christmas cards, and feasting upon a glorious goose came to America from Olde Englande.

In a re-creation of a kitchen that would have served German pioneers in Texas in the mid-ninteenth century, right, hand-embroidered shelf trim, brought out at the holidays, decorates a pie safe constructed in a rustic version of the German Biedermeier style. Preserves put up throughout the harvest season were tied with cheesecloth caps to adorn the shelves. Foods, both preserved and fresh, have long been signs of hospitality and equated with gift-giving.

To comply with the purely American infatuation with Santa's sleigh-bearers, a pair of rustic woodcarvings emulating his trusty reindeer were positioned, left, beside a barn in rural Pennsylvania so that they could greet all Christmas visitors. The little evergreens growing nearby were gussied up with maypole-style ribbons, which dance merrily in the frosty air.

Pioneer ingenuity inspired decorations created with local flora and especially greens such as the cedar in this kitchen window, left, in the Pioneer Museum in Texas. Here sprays of the aromatic green were pinned along a beam as a frothy valance; the valance was then punctuated by strings of cranberry and clusters of nandina berries. A butter churn and a graniteware pitcher and lidded casserole were set upon the sill.

In a parlor, opposite, in the same museum, a room-height branch of cedar tree was upended in a pot in lieu of a tree. It was hung only with cookies, some shaped like hearts and others like red-hatted gnomes—each tied securely to its branch by ribbon. In earlier times, candles would have been lit, but today this practice is banned because of the fire hazard. Nonetheless, it looks lovely to have real candles on the tree, and their unburned wicks set up a perky counterpoint to the gnomes' hats.

One Christmas tradition that has endured since Roman times is that of giving to the needy; preparing baskets of food and toys for distribution to hospitals and churches—or directly to the homes of those less fortunate—is a time-honored ritual, and representative of a disposition to generosity. Gatherings such as caroling, which had originated in the thirteenth century in England, have also long fostered a feeling of community spirit; sleigh rides and hay rides, church sing-a-longs, and suppers following the Christmas Pageant are all seasonal pleasures many communities look forward to each year to reinforce feelings of friendship and sharing. Today, when we consider—and re-enact—these longstanding rituals, we indulge in a nostalgia for what we remember as a simpler time and a simpler life in our nation. These recollections warm our hearts and they function—perhaps in a somewhat sentimental manner—to romanticize our roots, but: why not? The fantasy of the perfect Christmas is what makes the holiday live—a fantasy of joy and love and hope that, now and forever, is what we want to believe and cherish as the reality of this beloved celebration. We crave this belief; this faith is what nourishes us yearly and what binds us together as a nation and, after all, what makes us all Americans in spirit and kind.

Christmas cards, millions of them, are dispersed across America and overseas every year during December. The famous dictum, Merry Christmas and Happy New Year, was coined by Britisher Thomas Cole in 1843 when he created the first card, which also depicted a family celebration. Within a half dozen years, greeting cards had become enormously popular in England. In Boston, in 1874, lithographer Louis Prang produced the first greeting cards for sale in America, and by the 1890s card-sending was firmly established as an annual rite in this country—one that later burgeoned with the advent of Hallmark and other card companies, opposite.

On eastern Long Island, twin evergreen wreaths with pine cones and jaunty red bows, above, extend classic greetings of the season. Bows for wreaths should be made of fabric that will not run when wet with snow or rain.

hat is more joyous than sharing the absolute wonder of the season with family and friends—especially with children. No matter how many years pass, each Christmas when the tree is up and the lights are turned on for the first time I am a child again—filled with childlike wonder at the dazzling sight of so many twinkling lights.

CHAPTER TWO

THE HOMES OF CHRISTMAS

LIVING ROOMS THAT WELCOME

A fire. A tree. Stockings. Presents. Santa Claus is coming. . . . Such are the enticements that draw family and friends to the living room at Christmas time. This room most marvelously and truly "lives" up to its name at this time of year, conjuring up a spirit of magic and well-being, along with conviviality and conversation. Decorating the house for the holidays often starts here, with the placement of the biggest, tallest, fattest, most perfect tree. And once the tree has taken root, as it were, compatible greens are cut and arranged to fill out the scheme. There is no surface nor aperture that will not benefit from a snip or garland or branch or swag of pine. Holly and cedar, mistletoe and magnolia, eucalyptus and laurel, and other fresh or dried leaves and blooms add their impact, and may team up with traditional holiday plants such as poinsettia or narcissus. Candles echo fire flame, and stockings repeat the colors in a favorite quilt or homespun fabric draped over a table or the back of a sofa or chair. Wreaths at the window and electric candles placed on each sill send greetings out over the lawn, and conversely, pull a sparkle of the outdoors right inside for the enjoyment of one and all. Everyone can get into the decorating act: children can trim the bottommost branches of the tree while Dad tiptoes to place the star or angel on top. Stringing up popcorn and cranberry strands is a family project all can share, perhaps while listening to favorite carols and other holiday music on the radio, or watching one of the perennially offered Christmas movies on the TV.

Anticipation builds as visitors approach the living room, opposite, and within, its traditional Christmas tree. A bouquet of eucalyptus is gathered in a wide tartan ribbon in the hallway washstand. Beyond the soft pink wing chair the mantel is hung with evergreen and cranberry garlands. More garlands have been added, with popcorn strings, to the tree.

A custom-built replica of a colonial homestead, above, centers its living room upon an enormous brick fireplace modeled after one at Historic Deerfield in Massachusetts. Stenciling the walls in a red and green design established an opportune color scheme, and one that is repeated dramatically in the use of apples suspended by green ribbon from the ceiling.

A *perky row of store-bought stockings,* top, *awaits Santa's bounty in front of a fireplace in a bed-and-breakfast in Connecticut; no guest is ignored, not even the cat! Snippets of fresh-cut holly dance along the mantel shelf and accentuate a grapevine* *wreath hanging just above. The wreath receives seasonal trim throughout the year, but none seems more festive than holly with all its berries intact.*

Everyday collectibles such as a salt-glazed stoneware jug, left, *become festive when introduced to some pine boughs and seasonal ornaments. Rosy-cheeked Santa is a bright companion for the earth-toned jug.*

In Minnesota, *above, a keeping
room was transformed into a
family room, to combine a
comfortable seating area by
the fire with a festive dining
area beyond. The room-high
Christmas tree acts as both
transition between and focus*

*for the two areas during the
holidays. Scented greens fill
wooden shoes, baskets
hanging from ceiling beams,
and jugs throughout the room,
adding their fragrance to that
wafting from cinnamon sticks
and pomanders. A gleaming
version of a child's favorite—a*

*paper garland—festoons the
tree; this one is made of
heavy gold foil, which is
counterbalanced by robust
strands of wooden cranberries
and a single string of
popcorn. A trio of homemade
painted wooden Santas stands*

*atop a chimney cupboard
from Iowa, and favorite
antique toys join new, boxed
gifts under the tree.*

Of all the regional celebrations of the holidays in the United States, none is more colorful than that of the Southwest, and especially New Mexico. When Christmas approaches, the way is lit by farolitos—outdoor lanterns fabricated of paper bags filled partway with sand and a candle set inside—as a symbolic reminder of the lighting of the way, by stars, for the Holy Family almost two thousand years ago. The Southwest Christmas combines elements of Native American crafts and culture with that of Mexico, with a healthy dose of European-inspired Americana thrown in for good measure. Wreaths, for instance, are crafted of local red and green chilies, although greenery wreaths are also featured.

The classic adobe dwelling indigenous to the area centers on the fireplace, just as it does elsewhere, but a uniquely constructed one—a curvaceous beehive-style corner oven called the kiva. And the tree might sport brilliantly painted cutout tin ornaments based on holy figures and barnyard beasts imported or copied from Mexican tree decorations. Huge bonfires of piñon burn and the aroma is as tantalizing a reminder of the season as pine might be, say, in Maine or Massachusetts.

In a newly constructed adobe house near Santa Fe, the owners took liberties with color, painting a wall bright blue in part to highlight their annual Christmas tree, above. The evergreen stands sturdily against the wall, its ornaments a combination of chubby chilis in papier-mâché and homespun dolls; red-chili lights stand in for standard white twinklers. Stockings are hung by the chimney with care but, in this case, the fireplace is a new kiva. All the furniture in the room came from Mexico and exhibits an exuberance of line as well as a spirited attention to carved detail. A Mexican serape was folded on the bench in lieu of a cushion, and a folk painting fills another wall.

A candlestick angel from Mexico, opposite above, was handcrafted of clay and left uncolored; similar angels are often rendered in smaller versions to be hung as tree ornaments. A hand-painted miniature crèche, right, appears both whimsical and serious, with the usual panoply of Nativity characters—Mary, Joseph, the Babe, and Wise Men.

THE WARMTH OF THE HEARTH

Because of its life-giving warmth, the fire has been the central focus of the home since antiquity, and thus has always been associated with celebration, joy, and hope for renewal. From earliest times, therefore, the fire's surround was the recipient of decorative attention.

During the holidays, a cozy hearth acts like a magnet, drawing one and all to its embrace, and adorning the fireplace is a time-honored ritual. The decoration may complement the decor in your room or it can be treated as a single, fabulous decorative element to make a statement all on its

A long, feathery garland of balsam, opposite, cascades right onto the floor from the mantel and is accentuated by a feather tree and folk art sandpiper. Two potted juniper bushes flank the hearth and, as gifts to the garden, can be transplanted once the ground thaws in early spring.

Eucalyptus leaves, right, threaded together in a long strand and punctuated with dried pomegranates and cinnamon sticks, swag gracefully across an antique paneled wall, which was installed around a new fireplace. The overscaled and luxurious wreath hanging under the swag was constructed of laurel, dried hydrangea blooms, and lunaria, also known as the honesty plant.

35

own. Mix and match stockings and garlands, wreaths and candles, and collectibles for your own personal signature. The mantel can be draped with bits of antique fabric: velvet or brocade, laces and doilies. Favorite Christmas cards and ornaments too precious or fragile for the tree will have prominent safety on the mantel. Pretty boxes with jewel-like hard candies and pyramids of oranges, grapefruits, lemons, and limes bring extra color. Winter pot-pourris and bouquets of dried flowers are fragrant reminders of the summer just past. A quick, ever-lasting decoration is a yellow-ware or stoneware bowl heaped with dozens of pine cones.

Many years ago, quantities of walnuts and almonds in their shells were gilded with gold leaf and displayed on the mantel (and hung from the tree as well). And for those who still want to believe that the best things come in small packages, tiny, enticing, gaily wrapped presents can await their new owners just above the fireplace. Whatever you chose to adorn your fireplace, be sure to arrange any decoration so that it hangs at an adequate remove from the heat of the flame.

Extravagantly yet inexpensively decorated for Christmas Eve and Day, a natural oak mantel, above, wears a crown of fresh fruit and hemlock. Red and green grapes, pears, and lady apples are arranged on the evergreens by positioning the larger fruits first, then filling in with tiny lady apples. Fruit will keep a soft glow longer if it is misted once or twice a day with fresh water.

In a living room in the Green Mountains of Vermont, a colonial-blue fireplace, opposite, is the setting for an interesting collection of decorations. The trio of paper angels, hovering on a bed of pine boughs and baby's breath, is from Germany; the fragile red-and-white striped stockings are carefully hung beneath the angels each year. The garland under the mantel is accented with clusters of pears and berries at each end, and in the center, a stuffed bird.

Christmas is a time of favorite things both past and present. It's funny how a sight, or a sound, or even a smell can trigger a memory.

A happy
New - Year

A MERRY
CHRISTMAS

FAMILY CHRISTMAS DINING

All great festivals center on offerings of food. With the bounty-laden table as a focal point, the dining room naturally collects everyone together to share a menu lovingly prepared to celebrate the season. Therefore, the dining room, which may be virtually ignored the rest of the year, comes into its own and shines with a special radiance at Christmas. Decorations and trimmings such as garlands or wreaths and even a tree may be appropriately reiterated here, as a refrain or complement to the living room decor. The centerpiece for the room, of course, will be the table and how it is set. Be it for a buffet or sit-down dinner, the tabletop is like a theater in miniature or a gift for the senses. Pull out all the stops and bring out all your finery; this is the time to polish the sterling and iron best linens, to light the candles, and to serve and eat from fine china. Casual settings are appreciated, naturally enough, for informal festivities such as toddies after caroling or ice skating, or early breakfast before opening stockings on Christmas morning. The opportunities to make the dining room a magnificent and welcoming venue, therefore, are limited only by your capacity to entertain.

Set for a sweet-tooth's feast, opposite above, a dining room in western Massachusetts is festooned in garlands of pine sprinkled with bay laurel and popcorn, punctuated every few inches or so with a ripe cranberry.

Paper chains, red apples, and pine boughs were tied together to form a luxurious garland, opposite below, for an eighteenth-century cupboard in a California dining room. Primed for an orgy of gift-wrapping, the table is piled with baskets, which handily organize all the supplies.

In historic Westerfield House in Illinois, above, the dining room boasts an 1840s cupboard with an extensive pewter collection. At Christmas, the owners select decorations that will play up the patina of this dinnerware. Building on a large pewter tray, a pyramid of apples and pine is crowned with a majestic pineapple. Pomanders with red ribbons and red candles in holders continue the color theme.

41

A dining room in Pennsylvania, left, appropriately painted and stenciled in Christmas red and green, is garlanded and wreathed for the holidays with simple, unadorned pines. A trickle of pretty ribbon, clusters of kumquats, holly sprigs, a few bows, and candle glow are all that is needed to further foster merriment around a gift-laden table. Packages for guests are stacked nearby in a wing chair.

The dining room of a log home in Tennessee, above, is the setting for the family's ritual holiday entertaining. In their handsome cupboard, salt-glazed pottery is surrounded by bright red bittersweet. Antique Christmas blocks make an annual appearance.

HOLIDAY CUPBOARD DRESSING

The centerpiece of many a country-style living room, keeping room, dining room, and kitchen—and even a bedroom or hall—is a grand and wonderful cupboard, or even a couple of cupboards. Oftentimes the cupboard hoards a family's most treasured collections, be they ceramics or homespuns or baskets or toys. The cupboard, therefore, serves as a primary focus for a room, and, as such, could continue to do so just as easily at Christmas time. The holiday decorations for a cupboard can complement a total room scheme—or they can, indeed, set the style, tone, and mood for the entire space. Greens, Christmas tree balls and ornaments, wreaths, garlands, and even tiny, contained candles all enhance the sturdy lines and silhouette of a cupboard and its built-in shelving. All decorations, though, should be slightly smaller or narrower in scale than those that frame the doorway, say, or a mantelpiece; you don't want to overwhelm a cupboard, or any piece of furniture for that matter, with its decorations. Favorite collectibles such as toys can be prettied up with bows made of thin ribbon in plain colors or cheerful Christmas plaids. And don't overlook knobs; dangle a tiny wreath or ornament or greeting card from a door or drawer to say welcome.

In an inn in upstate New York, a pie safe, opposite far left, attributed to Shaker manufacture was decked out with a variety of toys and decorations, including a cranberry string punctuated with popcorn. A gingerbread house, dripping with sugary icicles, perches on the safe; a reindeer is poised upon the chimney to aid Santa's escape. Two little Shaker-style stockings hang on the door of the safe, just for show.

The safest candles to set on any shelf or in a cupboard, opposite near right, are votives because they are harbored and protected by thick glass. Votives look equally pretty placed at random among collectibles, or positioned in tidy rows. A tuft of pine or holly is the only additional decoration that is necessary as a foil to the candle glow.

An eighteenth-century stepback cupboard, right, bearing the residue of its original blue paint, was draped with a lush garland woven of white pine entwined with bunches of heather. There's no mistaking the holiday the cupboard was decorated for—what with the four giant printshop blocks spelling out the season: Y U L E. A pair of polished apples and freshly molded beeswax candles add bright color and a hint of fragrance to the scene.

CANDLE GLOW

The flicker and glow of candle flame shimmeringly evoke myriad impressions that are at once sensuous and spiritual. One of the yearly celebrations of the season is the December 13th Feast of St. Lucia, when Swedish girls sing a carol honoring the popular saint's memory while wearing crowns of four candles in their hair. The candles of Chanukah and those of Christmas also inspire holy meditation. But candles, too, simply and effectively add tender warmth to every part of the house. March a series of fat pillars along a mantel or a dining table, or cluster them atop a coffee table. These chunky candles can be dressed in palm leaves caught up with a wide tartan ribbon, or flanked by cinnamon sticks tied in place with twine. Similarly, pine boughs can be tied to candles with a length of gold cord. If you prefer elegant tapers, group them in a shallow bowl for a lovely halo of candlelight. Fragrant candles of bayberry or hollyberry add a special scent to the air, especially in rooms without wood-burning fireplaces. And votive candles in each window will wink a greeting to all who pass by.

A *soft glow emanates from three pear-shaped candles, opposite, set out on a dining room cupboard. Baby hemlocks in terra-cotta pots are kept from drying out with a cover of sphagnum moss. Gold balls are made by gluing nuts in their shells to Styrofoam forms, then spray-painting.*

C*andles gleaming in a pair of rare coiled hogscrapers, right, and a brass candlestick light an ancestral portrait and a burl bowl brimful of lady apples. Using salvaged candlestubs suits the proportion of the candlesticks and looks more authentically antique.*

Candles in general are a festive yet easy way to ornament the home. In Victorian times, it was popular to add tapers directly to the Christmas tree using candleholders specially designed to hold them upright. To give your tree a romantic, old-fashioned look, you might consider hunting down these timeless ornaments for use in your tree or using reproduction holders. But don't light the candles—use them purely for visual impact; simply complement them with tiny white lights to simulate the glow of candlelight.

Teaming up a collection of red wooden candlesticks, above, with matching tapers presents a luminous display. At the same time it proves again the steadfast design rule that objects of disparate shapes will be unified through color.

Votive candles redolent with the fragrance of cooking spices, left, cast their sparkle into a pair of champagne flutes and beckon revelers to toast in a "Happy New Year!"

Many American vernacular Christmas customs actually originated in other lands. In the Southwest, residents adapt the Mexican custom of lighting lanterns on Christmas Eve in a unique manner. Southwestern farolitos, or "little lanterns," are created by filling small paper bags with a sand base and placing votive candles squarely in the center of each. Throughout the towns and cities of New Mexico, hundreds of farolitos line sidewalks and squares and sit atop adobe walls.

Once lit, the candles create a soft, ethereal glow and are most effective when used en masse. Line a walkway leading to your home with farolitos, beginning at the sidewalk and extending along the front steps, right up to the door. Farolitos also look stunning grouped on a porch banister or placed atop a garden wall. They can be used inside the home in an open area, such as a walkway or along flights of steps. Farolitos displayed in a bay window are a warm greeting to holiday visitors.

The adobe walls of a house in Santa Fe, top, seem to have been designed for farolitos. Here they line a path to the owner's house. The cheery lanterns are lit every day as the afternoon begins to fade and heighten the drama of the New Mexico sunset.

Farolitos can be used as effectively in more northerly locations, above, especially along a sheltered entry.

THE CHRISTMAS KITCHEN

Delicious smells, delicious tastes: from the first bite into the Thanksgiving turkey through the last sip of New Year's Champagne, the kitchen pulsates with culinary sensations. Baking, roasting, simmering, and stewing all motivate heart-to-hand enthusiasm and energy, and decorations to match. Decorations inspired by or created from foods such as cookies or pomanders or popcorn chains are especially appropriate— though they may be picked off by passersby who "just want to test and taste" them as the season progresses. A single note of caution though: display poisonous plants such as mistletoe or poinsettia, which do shed berries and leaves, in other rooms of the house, where there is no chance that they will infect food.

"Keeping room" is an apt description for a large and expansive kitchen in a log home in Tennessee, right. The great fireplace keeps the house warm, keeps foods ready for a glorious dessert buffet, and even keeps stockings close to Santa's preferred entry chute. Because of its robust size, the room easily accommodates a large harvest table—it's eight feet long—as well as a wood stove. A frail but resilient little pine stands in a bed of twisted Spanish moss in a firkin on the table, next to a pair of teddy pals. A grapevine wreath over the fireplace was accentuated with dried hydrangeas, ribbon, and straw bells.

Doing up a kitchen in holiday finery can be as simple as tying sprightly bows here and there on favorite collectibles and on the outstretched arms of a chandelier, opposite. *Christmas towels and coordinating linens and a puffy tree, some felt-hatted, yarn-bearded Santas tugged atop wine, soda, or cider as bottle "caps," and a scattering of greens and pine cones contribute extra cheer.*

Harboring an abundance of gifts of food, a bright white Connecticut kitchen, right above, relies on natural light and fragrant flowers to elicit a spirit of good will. A narrow garland tied up with ribbon sets off the multi-paned windows like a valance, but never inhibits sun from streaming onto the hardy narcissus and companion winter-blooming plants. In December, the owner's bright-red spatterware pots become an inadvertent Christmas decoration.

Mauve, an unexpected color for Christmas decor, proves exceptionally charming in a New Jersey kitchen, right, because it picks up on the room's painted woodwork as well as the subtler tones in a prized collection of Staffordshire plates. A lightweight cotton blanket covers a table set for a convivial eggnog party.

hristmas is a time of special aromas, of tangerines and cakes baking and cookies cooling on the kitchen counter. There are the smells of logs burning in the fireplace, pungent evergreens that perfume every room in the house, and the spicy fragrance of cloves and cinnamon and nutmeg boiling gently in a kettle on the stove.

Tablesettings that Celebrate

Because the season of celebration extends from Thanksgiving through Chanukah and Christmas to the New Year, many opportunities present themselves for indulging in imaginative settings for the table. Buffet or banquet? Supper or cocktails? The tabletop, in a very real and joyful sense, becomes a stage for culinary triumphs, but how it is set will also demonstrate just how much the host honors and cares for each guest. There are countless small ways to say welcome, come partake, let's eat and talk. Pretty cards may identify each place at table, but a setting may be singled out, too, with an ornament or miniature toy, a poem, limerick, or greeting, a child's drawing, a

candy, or. . .the list goes on. A gracious centerpiece may be set upon the table to remain in place throughout the season. A folk art Santa Claus, for instance, could hold court, with or without a sleigh and sack of little gifts, all December long. This is the season to bring out precious heirloom dinnerware from under wraps in a trunk or the attic, for best porcelains or fine china, gleaming crystal, and polished-to-a-glow sterling assume a special aura and importance when used to continue a time-honored family tradition. A holiday table without candlelight is difficult to imagine! And do not forget to offer a lovely wine or Champagne or hearty cider, sweetmeats or mints or nonpareils.

How to Make a Bell Ornament

For an intimate supper, opposite left, both table and chairs may be pulled up right next to the fire and the Christmas stew ladled straight from the pot. To flatter a meal such as this, keep decorations as low key as possible: drape a length of red felt—cut and "bordered" with pinking shears—diagonally across the table, and add a robust poinsettia in a tub. Tuck away a gift or two to open after the meal as an unexpected pleasure.

A diminutive beeswax bear, above, made especially for the occasion from an antique candy mold, rests atop a sprig of balsam, centered on a dishwasher-safe, pewter-like plate. To protect the plaid blanket that serves as a tablecover, a washable placemat was inserted underneath the tablesetting.

Tablesettings become truly memorable when guests are given a lasting souvenir such as the quilt Christmas bell above. The bells are simply made from quilt scraps and remnants and finished with a tiny bell and top bow.

To make a bell, draw and cut out a pattern about 6 inches high on heavy brown paper. For each ornament, cut two bells from quilt scraps (or cut one from quilt and the other from a complementary fabric for backing). Place right-sides together. Loop a 2⅝ inch length of narrow grosgrain ribbon through a jinglebell; center the ribbon along the bottom edge of the ornament, with the bell in the direction of the ornament's top. Sew the ornament ⅝ inch from the edges, leaving a 2-inch opening at the top center. Carefully turn the ornament right-side-out and lightly fill with polyester batting. Slip-stitch the opening at the top. With an 8- to 10-inch length of medium-wide ribbon, tie a loop and a bow; sew the ribbon to the top of the ornament.

THE INVITING ENTRY

How to Decorate with Garlands

For the child—and the child in us—the stairway offers the most provocative perch during the holidays. From this tempting vantage point all comings and goings of gifts and wishes, kisses and dreams, can be cozily surveyed. And so the staircase, which might receive scant attention the rest of the year, should not be overlooked as a backdrop for companionable decorations. Because, of course, stairs ascend by the dozen, consider showing them off with multiples of one cherished object—for instance, stone crocks or teddy bears—conferring one prize to each tread. Or guide the way, step by step, with holiday plants such as miniature yews, poinsettias, or even tiny pines. The banister is obviously the suitable foil for a long stretch of garland, but the rail can be accented, too, with ornaments suspended between the balusters, or ribbons tied on with bows.

A sinuous swirl of balsam spills down a stair, opposite, and then is caught at the base of the newel post in a flourish. Striped grosgrain ribbons secure the garland to the stair rail; a matching bow centers the pine bough over the front door. More pine needles were sewn into a fragrant and "merry" pillow.

Garlands are one of the easiest and most versatile decorations to make. Virtually any type of evergreen can be used—pine, juniper, hemlock, boxwood, lemon leaves—and the look can be spare or lush, as you prefer. To make a garland, wrap greens together at the stem with lightweight wire; continue adding boughs at the stem-end, tying each piece securely with wire. Decorations for garlands are endless: ribbons; dried flowers such as hydrangeas or baby's breath; lacy paper doilies tied up with satin ribbons; cellophane-wrapped hard candies; fresh or faux fruits; tiny teddy bears or rag dolls; lightweight papier-mâché Santas such as those above. Or drill holes in the shells of walnuts, pecans, and almonds to attach them with wire; for a richer look, dust nuts with gold spray paint. If your garland is on kitchen stairs, decorate it with biscuits and breadsticks; a garland on the porch outside can be studded with birdseed bells. Strings of tree lights, tiny and white for delicate garlands or bold and bright for more robust ones, are the final touch.

SEASONAL BEDROOMS

Even if most of the festivities of the holidays take place in the traditionally public rooms of the house, this does not mean that the bedroom be overlooked as a beautiful venue for decoration—and even for celebration. Many families with small children congregate on the parental bed early Christmas morning with stuffed stockings in hand, ready to unwrap their mysterious surprises before breakfast. And, of course, all the pre-Christmas secrecy of gift-wrapping often takes place in this sanctuary, away from prying or curious eyes. A small tree—or even a big one—might find a happy niche in this room, swagged in ribbon or tricked out with little nibbles to spur on the gift-wrapping marathon. Heirloom toys from parental childhoods could tuck in around the base of the tree, or, decked out with holly or other greens and trim, assume a place of importance upon the dresser, bedside table, or window sill. Four-poster beds are especially receptive to decoration. Green garlands or bands of lace may twine around posters and across the top; a wreath can be suspended from upper cross-bars with wide ribbons; just for the season, bedhangings can be coiled with strings of tiny white lights. An electric candle in each win-

dow will wink all night long, and, on Christmas Eve, who knows?—a tiny surprise treat might appear, like magic, beneath every pillow in the house. If your house has no chimney for Santa Claus to shimmy down, stockings can be hung with just as much care at the head or foot of each bed. And for each impatient child, an advent calendar on the bedroom wall will help to mark off the days that remain before the big holiday.

A tiny St. Nick stands
in for a shepherd, opposite,
to watch benignly over a
woolly flock in front of a
scenic landscape conveniently
sized to scale near a pretty
papered bandbox. A few snips
of pine extend the scene right
across the dresser top.

In a one-room cottage,
above, a cedar placed at the
foot of a homespun-covered
bed is wound with a casual
ribbon, which unfurls around
a collection of gaily painted
glass ornaments. More cedar
frames the photo portrait.

In a little boy's room, above, a tiny, slightly eccentric sapling was placed right next to the bed, to coax sweet dreams and festive thoughts from the room's occupant, especially on Christmas Eve. Plush teddies harbor their own fantasies as they snuggle together on the blanket chest, and a spiffy new bat signals presents that may be waiting under the tree downstairs.

A swag-and-jabot of greens was fastened inside the window frame, opposite above, in an under-the-eaves bedroom in Vermont. A lemon studded with cloves hangs from a fat ribbon behind the center of the swag, adding color and aroma to the window dressing. Special Christmasy quilts cover the bed, and, at its foot, antique toys are reminders of holidays past.

Baskets of many sizes and shapes collect pine cones and other natural delights culled from the fields and woods in a country bedroom, right. Gifts may also be secreted in these rustic portable carryalls, ready to take downstairs to the tree on the Big Day. Fat columnar candles and a little stocking beckon Santa to this hearth.

DECORATIONS BY NATURE

Authentic, inexpensive, readily available, and truly beautiful—decorations of natural materials, whether they are plants, fruits and vegetables, or herbs and spices, are wonderfully appropriate for the holidays. Gather a fat sheaf of tall wheat, symbolizing the fruited plains, and tie it up with a thick velvet ribbon. Stand this on the floor alongside the stairs or make a pair to flank the fireplace hearth. A graceful sheaf of dried lavender, on the other hand, can be wrapped with a cord of silver or gold to rest on a bedside table. Abundance can elevate the mundane into the extraordinary: a great rustic dough bowl piled with tangerines is effective on a keeping room sideboard. Throughout the house, bowls brimming with fresh fruits or pine boughs or potpourris bring life to the most neglected corners. Tucking decorations into the nooks and crannies of the house will cultivate Christmas spirit through the season.

Set on an oak sidetable, a beautifully simple arrangement, above left, of long-needle pine boughs, red tree ornaments, and cinnamon sticks will last two or three weeks.

Wreaths of pine cones and dried flowers, above right, combine with bowls of walnuts and cranberries and pine, apples, cinnamon sticks, and pine cones on a dining room sideboard.

Life imitates art, opposite above, as the centuries-old practice of making pomanders is depicted in an oil painting while underneath lemons and tangerines are aged and displayed in antique copper bowls.

A rustic, shallow wood bowl, opposite below, is filled with rose potpourri and a variety of pomanders.

How to Prepare Pomanders

At one time, a pomander was a mixture of aromatic spices carried in a perforated bag that was believed to ward off infection. Today, it is the name we use for citrus fruit that has been studded with cloves. Oranges are most commonly used, but grapefruit, blood oranges, tangerines, lemons, limes, and even kumquats are also wonderful pomanders. Each fruit emits its own fragrance, and you may want to experiment to determine which you like best.

MAKES 3 POMANDERS
1 medium-size orange
5 1.2-ounce packages whole cloves
1 lemon
1 kumquat
1 tablespoon powdered orrisroot (see note)
1 tablespoon ground cinnamon
1 tablespoon ground allspice
1½ teaspoons ground nutmeg
Narrow ribbons

1. Using bamboo skewer, toothpick, or ice pick, puncture skin of orange and insert clove. Repeat in rows as close together as possible to cover fruit completely with cloves. If desired, leave narrow crossed sections of skin unstudded in order to fit a ribbon around the fruit once it dries. Repeat the studding process on lemon and kumquat.

2. In plastic bag, combine orrisroot, cinnamon, allspice, and nutmeg. Roll clove-studded fruit in orrisroot mixture; shake off excess. Wrap in tissue paper and allow to age a few weeks in a dry place at room temperature.

3. Wrap ribbon around unstudded grooves in dried fruit. Tie pomander balls together, if desired.

Note: Orrisroot is available in drugstores and craft and hobby stores.

WINTER WREATHS

When hung upon a front door, a wreath offers the first greeting of the season. In fact, the wreath is one of the oldest symbols of celebration and esteem. In ancient Greece, young lovers suspended wreaths on each others' doorways to signal their affections. In ancient Greece, too, athletes and poets alike were awarded coronets of laurel to signify excellence. Laurel is just one of the greens traditionally associated with the holiday wreath; other familiar ones include pine and spruce. Consider also rhododendron or boxwood, magnolia or even mosses. To craft a wreath, you need a sturdy, doughnut-shaped support. Wire frames and Styrofoam rings are commercially available, but you can form your own from chicken wire or grapevine stems or wire-wrapped straw. The rule of thumb: Make it as lush and full as possible.

On a grain-painted jam cupboard, left, a simple homemade wreath of freshly cut pine interspersed with a few sprigs of holly, berries, and lady apples gently frames a miniature house and subtly echos faintly defined greenery painted on the owner's collection of nineteenth-century bandboxes.

An ordinary pine wreath, above, becomes special with the addition of a garland of red tartan ribbon and an energetic teddy, also in a tartan tie.

Inside a door, a grapevine wreath
with sachets.

Outside, a rugged grapevine
wreath with bittersweet.

Against a red door, a wreath
of classic laurel.

An energetic wreath of dried
heather, against a quilt.

Dried pomegranates set like
jewels in a green crown.

On a boxwood wreath, apple
slices preserved with shellac.

A trio of wreaths of dried
crabapples.

Clusters of bittersweet berries
in a grapevine wreath.

CHAPTER THREE

THE
TREES
OF
CHRISTMAS

THE NATIONAL EVERGREEN

•

A TREE FOR EVERY ROOM

•

ANTIQUE ORNAMENTS

•

NATURAL TRIMS

•

WHIMSICAL DECORATIONS

•

ORNAMENTS FROM CRAFTSPEOPLE

•

FABRIC ORNAMENTS TO MAKE

•

PAPER HEARTS TO MAKE

•

COOKIES AS ORNAMENTS

•

COOKIE ORNAMENTS TO BAKE

THE NATIONAL EVERGREEN

From the utter stillness of the pine forest to rooms alive with the music of good cheer, evergreen trees come by the millions each year to become spectacular symbols of the American holiday. Balsam, with its longlasting fragrance, was our first Christmas tree. Today, regional varieties abound—Grand Fir in the Northwest, the Monterey of the Southeast and Southwest, Balsam in the Midwest, and Spruce in the Northeast. Scotch Pine, Norway Spruce, Blue Spruce, Douglas Fir, and Eastern White Pine are all popular trees, if a bit more expensive at the market.

Trees last longer in cooler rooms, so if you buy your tree early, you may want to keep it outdoors or on an unheated porch until decorated. To extend the life of your tree as long as possible, give the trunk a new cut before installing the tree stand. Christmas trees need plenty of fresh, cool water—sometimes even more than once a day—to keep them from drying out, especially if they're in warm, dry rooms.

Nature is still the most accomplished decorator of all, as a majestic tree, opposite, demonstrates. Enrobed with a blanket of just-fallen snow, the trees on this property present a winter tableau prettier than any Christmas card.

Set in front of a lace-curtained window, a formal tree, right, echoes the room's delicate decoration with dried Queen Anne's lace, antique Santas, and white candle lights. Holly has been used for additional decoration in the stencil above the window and as tie-backs on the curtain.

A Tree for Every Room

In the Pioneer Museum of Fredericksburg, Texas, a tabletop tree, above, has been set alongside the screen door, much as it would have been a century ago. The tree is set in a sand-filled graniteware farm bucket, and set on a table draped with a crochet tablecover .

Because the American landscape was—in the main—luxuriant with evergreens, the custom of cutting a full-grown tree, rather than merely settling for the tabletop version celebrated in Europe, caught on early and soon became a tradition unique to this country. In its guise as a bearer of gifts, the tree was awarded the most auspicious location in the house, usually the "best" room or front parlor. To surprise the children, the tree was set in place in secret—shielded from curious peek-a-boos—and only then revealed, in all its glory, on the eve of the 24th or on Christmas Day. Today, flexibility is the norm, and many houses boast not only one tree, but often more, with each granted its own precious place of honor. The grandest tree still claims the prime spot, usually close to the hearth in the living room or family room. But trees both big and diminutive may happily reside in any other room—at the end of a bed, perhaps, or on a dining table or in a cozy kitchen corner.

The Palladian windows of a family room in Connecticut, opposite, are a backdrop for a magnificent balsam pine. This great tree has been hung with hundreds of colorful country ornaments and tiny white lights. At its side, a tree strictly for the children, decorated with less-fragile bows, attracts its own pile of presents underneath.

Trees tucked into corners of the house or placed in odd rooms are meant to be "discovered" by holiday visitors, adding to the festive quality of the holiday. The dining room side table is a good focal point for a plucky little tree, opposite, delicate enough to be set in an antique Merry Christmas stand. Because it is set out of harm's way, the tree has been hung with the family's most fragile, most treasured ornaments. The stairway landing, right, is also a dramatic setting for a tree. A row of rich red poinsettias draws the eye toward the tree, on which fat but almost weightless dried hydrangeas rest.

ANTIQUE ORNAMENTS

Radiant with multi-colored miniature lights, a live pine, opposite, securely planted in a galvanized bucket, gleans additional sparkle from a collection of German-made glass ornaments, which were tied onto its branches with lengths of tartan grosgrain ribbon. The elongated glass ornaments were formed by pulling at the molten glass while it was still red-hot. Other balls were pushed in on their surfaces to create concave hollows for extra visual appeal. Strings of glass beads dangle around the tree. Antique toys such as the 1930s tin roadster-style automobile mingle with gifts at the base of the tree.

The cherished ornaments we consider antique today are actually barely a century old, if that. For years most were imported—as was the concept of the decorated tree—from Germany. In the late 1800s German ornaments, almost all of which were made of blown glass, captivated the hearts of Americans who admired their delicacy and luminous appearance. For a while, though, many people could afford only one or two ornaments a year, but Mr. Woolworth of five-and-dime fame and other entrepreneurs soon saw an extraordinary opportunity for sales, and they imported literally hundreds of thousands of glass ornaments each season. Glass balls and icicles were early favorites, but soon the range of designs seemed limitless, and included animal and bird shapes, fruits, houses, and of course, Santas. Other antique ornaments which swiftly caught on were made from tin, wood, wax, paper, cardboard, and papier-mâché. Some trees ended up so covered one could no longer see branch or needles.

The glass ball, above left, is still the most sought-after ornament; whether it is old or new matters not. Strings of glass beads repeat the shape of the glass ball a thousandfold. Early glass bead strands were crafted in Czechoslovakia and often interspersed with other shaped beads such as stars with miniature spheres. Cottonwood ornaments also enjoyed great popularity; lambs, above right, wearing real sheepskin coats, can be hung or may, instead, gather in a flock on a shelf.

At the turn of the century, Americans, infatuated with the nostalgic appeal of scrapbooks, bought countless pictures to fill these at every opportunity. Ornament makers, capitalizing on the craze, created a cornucopia of delightful "scraps" for the tree. These die-cut lithographed ornaments, opposite top left, were seasonal sell-outs and included angels and cherubs and Santa Clauses as well as other images such as sleighs. Almost all of the handblown glass ornaments imported to the States before World War I disrupted production came from a single town in Germany — Lausha — where glassblowing had been a tradition. Glass ornaments were silvered inside, lacquered with color, and then touched up — all by hand. Many of the shaped ornaments, such as the bells and the Santa, opposite bottom left and right, were blown into a mold. A tender addition to the tree is the gift tag; the well-wisher's stocking, opposite top right, dates from 1910. Whatever the material, though, the themes remained, and remain today, common and sentimental — angels, babies, bears, and Father Christmas, right.

NATURAL TRIMS

Far from the tempting shops of the city, rural Christmas revelers would rely on trees cut from the nearby woods and trims fabricated inventively from simple country offerings, materials harvested from nature's bounty that were supplemented with sweet treats, cookies, and foods. The most natural of trimmings, of course, could be culled directly from woods or fields, garden plot or orchard, and these perfectly complemented the evergreen. Pine cones and chestnuts and walnuts left plain or gilded and bark were, and are, readily assimilated into the receptive greenery of fir or spruce or balsam. Apples of the edible variety— and their diminutive cousins the crabapple and the lady apple—and pears can be casually hung from their stems. Apples can be sliced, too, to make pretty dried bracelets for the tree. Dried flowers such as hydrangea and Queen Anne's lace, which can be used singly, and roses and lavender, which are usually massed in nosegays, are popular too. In the Southwest, dried chili peppers add pizazz and a dose of hot color. Bunches of bittersweet or hollyberries, with or without leaves, will punctuate the green with accents of color, too. Clumps of mistletoe may be used as well, but with caution, for mistletoe is extremely poisonous.

Natural trims look best when clustered thickly, as their abundant massing will effectively fill in any gaps between branches of a tree. Clusters can be strung together, too, to form generous and luxuriant garlands. Natural trims are often teamed with candles, but, again, candles should be of the clip-on electric variety; real candles are illegal in most states. In any case, candle drippings or flame could spark a fire, especially with natural trim, in a flash. In the old days a bucket of water and a sponge were kept on hand as an antidote to danger. Today it is best to comply with the law.

Pine cones in varying sizes, opposite, were wired together to form small wreaths with just the right diameter openings to slide securely over balsam branches. Clusters of berries were positioned on the tree to resemble garlands; as a variation they could have been dotted about all over the tree instead.

In a close-up of the same tree, above, a folk art sanderling—part of a covey of wild fowl alighted upon the branches—glances over its winged shoulder to the berry cluster garlands and cone wreaths. The array of birds, left unadorned in their own guileless beauty, enhances the natural theme.

Little nosegays of baby's breath, opposite, dapple a twinkling tree. Each nosegay was cut precisely to harmonize with compatibly scaled ornaments. Cranberry garlands sweep from branch to branch, adding arcs of red.

Long ago, popcorn used to be dyed in bright colors as a punchy accent to the tree, but today we would consider this rather garish indeed. And, after all, the candid white of the popped kernels presents such an attractive contrast to the deep green of the pine boughs. Another natural touch, above, to consider: tie ornaments onto the branches with plain twine or red country-store string.

All you need to create your own garlands of popcorn and cranberries, right, are the natural ingredients, a needle, and firm white thread—plus a healthy dose of patience and strong fingers.

WHIMSICAL DECORATIONS

There are as many ways to dress a tree as there are to clothe yourself. Although traditional ornaments are the norm, many "found objects" can dazzle a tree. Look around your house and challenge family members: what can we do to the tree this year to make it truly memorable? Could the tree, for instance, follow a color theme exhibiting ornaments all of the same hue? Or might it illustrate a nautical motif, with tiny boats and stars to steer them by? The tree can turn into a "canvas" for children's art—with hand-cut bells and stars and Santas and paper chains instead of garlands. Smaller, tabletop trees for private rooms of the house are ideal for thematic decoration—a kitchen tree hung with the cookie cutters themselves, a tree for the bedroom with sachets and lace handkerchiefs, even a bathroom tree with tiny pastel guest soaps. If you have roots in another culture, express your heritage by displaying ornaments and lights that speak that language. And, if you love to fantasize freely, hang whatever intrigues you upon your tree. Make your tree a personal and individual statement.

An utterly extravagant and sophisticated tabletop tree, above left, wears orchids as if they were jewels. Clusters of colored glass beads, lady apples, tiny white lights, and gilded pine cones make a truly unusual and distinctive tree, perfectly appropriate for a Christmas cocktail party.

For a miniature pine tree, above right, miniature decorations suffice. Tiny molds, replicas of grown-up kitchen collectibles, hang from extra-thin ribbons and are complemented by a single string of wooden beads, which mimic cranberries. The tree was set into a specially crafted birchbark stand.

A teepee-shaped tree of toy bears, opposite, was constructed around a Styrofoam cone bought at the dime store. The long-needled pine boughs and huggable collection of bears were tethered to the cone with florists' wire, and then strands of miniature twinkle lights were twisted around the cone to harness the bears to each other more securely.

ORNAMENTS FROM CRAFTSPEOPLE

Characters from storybooks have enchanted youngsters for generations, so ornaments based on beloved friends such as Pooh Bear, above left, are indubitably pleasing additions to the tree. A brilliant cardinal perched on a real twig not only perks up a branch but also introduces youthful birdwatchers to the art of elementary ornithological identification.

Making gifts, wrappings, trimmings, cards, and ornaments by hand—or purchasing them already crafted as expressions of sentiment and joy—draws upon a long history of American pioneer ingenuity and equally upon a simple and enduring theme: To give from the heart is to give from the hand. Before the Industrial Age, many communities had no option but to conserve precious materials such as fabric, and so holiday gifts, by neccessity, had to be practical: most were homemade. But inventive whimsies and toys would be mixed wherever possible to delight and surprise. The range of crafted ornaments is as rich and various as the myriad craftspeople of our nation. Regional and religious customs happily influence these kinds of ornaments and a good measure of human eccentricity plays to the American sense of humor. In this way, the American love of craft continues—and crafted ornaments are treasured, to become traditions in themselves.

The case clock, above right, with its cheerful face, was cut—as were the Pooh and the cardinal—from balsa wood, which was then painted. Cardboard would be suitable too; stiffness is the only prerequisite to durability.

All sorts of handmade, homemade ornaments mingle with store-bought finds, above, on a "user-friendly" tree. Every member of the family may add his or her own personal treat to the branches. A tiny, tidy square of needlepoint backed with felt and little stockings stitched up and stuffed with cotton batting make good use of odd bits of fabric, yarn, and ribbon in the sewing basket. Popcorn balls were constructed around Styrofoam balls and then red ribbons were attached for hanging. Always use sturdy materials so ornaments will last from year to year.

The simplest adornment for a tree, besides strands of white lights, is ribbon. Ribbons can be tied into bows, right, or threaded throughout the branches or hung from the crown of the tree, maypole-style, as streamers. Crocheted hearts impart a message of love—both to the season and to family and friends.

A *plump, perfectly shaped tree stands in the place of honor alongside the original fireplace in the keeping room of a 1760 colonial home in Connecticut, right. Each year, new ornaments are added to older handmade ones like the wood oranges and apples, crocheted stars, stuffed calico hearts and horses, and colorful lollipops tied with checked ribbon. Near the fireplace, over the stored firewood, an antique crèche is displayed in what was the Dutch oven. As works-in-progress, lady apples, above, will be tied with gold and ruby cord held in place by straight pins.*

npacking the ornaments
is like opening a box of
memories. Many of the
decorations bring to mind a
special time or place or
person. The tree will soon be
laden with ornaments collected
over the years, each with its
own story to tell. When
we have finished decorating,
the shining evergreen creates
a magic that we are never
too old to enjoy.

FABRIC ORNAMENTS TO MAKE

A *chubby little pine tree standing in front of an arched fireplace in a fieldstone house in Pennsylvania, left, was rigged out with a cheerful assortment of patchwork-style ornaments. Some were left flat, some were stuffed, and others have tiny secret pockets for candy and other special surprises.*

Although handmade ornaments may assume many guises, and may be made from many materials, the most beloved motifs for country Christmas trees may well be those adapted from patchwork quilts and sewn up, like them, from pretty fabric. Designs such as the basket, the star, and the heart are especially easy to cut out and sew; in fact, the same silhouettes would work both for an ornament and a design on a quilt block. Of course, a cookie or Santa Claus, or stocking, bell, or ball, can be stitched up following these same instructions—which offer no problem even to children, who can join in the fun of decorating the tree with their own handwork. Gather up snips and bits of fabric all year long and save them for your ornaments. One colorful and economical fabric to consider is felt, which is available in a range of bold colors and needs no hemming.

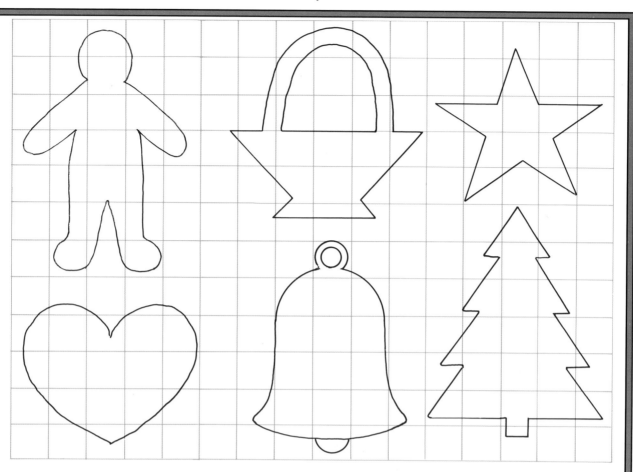

Make These Fabric Ornaments

Colorful tree ornaments can be stitched up in minutes from felt or fabric scraps. Felt is especially easy to work with because the edges don't fray, and it is available in a range of vivid colors. Kids will enjoy making these, too.

To begin, gather together scraps of felt, colorful printed fabrics (use firmly woven, light- to medium-weight ones to minimize fraying); ribbons, trims, and buttons; a small amount of polyester fiberfil or cotton batting; lightweight cardboard; and a pencil.

Make templates from the patterns above, enlarging them to scale. One square equals one inch. Transfer to the cardboard and cut out.

Sew gingerbread men, stars, baskets and other ornaments from felt; hearts can be made from felt or woven fabric. Arrange the templates on felt or fabric. Each ornament needs a front and back piece, so trace around the template twice. For fabric hearts, add ¼-inch seam allowance all around. Cut out the shapes.

On the front sections, applique details using fabric scraps or embroider details and messages. Remember that the back side will probably rest against the tree and not show. On that side you may want to stitch "Christmas" and the year. These ornaments can also be used as gift tags or labels.

For felt ornaments, place the front and back sections together, wrong-sides facing; hand-sew close to the edge, leaving a small opening for stuffing. Stuff lightly and sew closed. For woven-fabric ornaments, place the front and back wrong-sides facing and stitch a ¼-inch seam. Turn to the right side, stuff lightly, and sew the opening.

PAPER HEARTS TO MAKE

A folded paper, heart-shaped ornament that can be seen on many trees each Christmas came to our country from Denmark. The preparation of these hearts is as much a tradition there as the ornaments themselves. Before the tree is brought in, the family will gather, fold, and weave hearts, always in red and white, the colors of the Danish flag.

Here there is no end to the color—and pattern—combinations that you can choose. And there is no end to the ways the hearts can be used: on the tree, of course, but also on kitchen and bathroom cupboard knobs, on window frames and in doorways, on spindle-back chairs and bookcases, and especially to dress up pine and twig garlands, valances, and wreaths.

Nestled into evergreen boughs, paper hearts, in a variety of sizes, bring their own sweetness to the tree. When they are made of foil or paper that has a shiny finish, they reflect the tree lights beautifully.

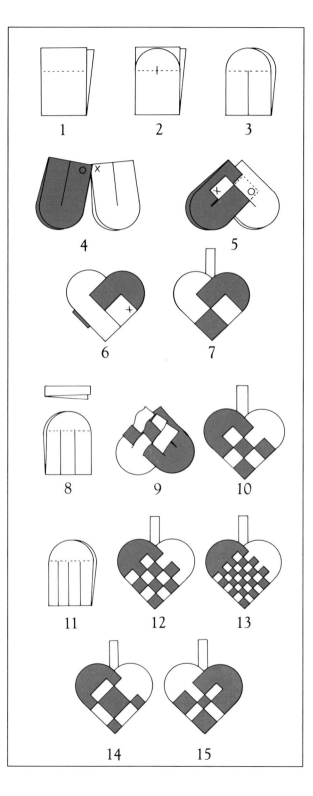

How to Make
Paper Hearts

1. For the basic paper heart, you will need two pieces of glazed paper, each three times as long as it is wide, each a different color. The folding and cutting instructions are the same for both pieces: fold each piece in half, colored side out. From the fold upwards, mark off a square (shown as broken line).

2. Taking the top of the square as the diameter, draw a semicircle above the square with a compass (or anything circular such as a drinking glass or cup). Cut off triangular portions.

3. In the two folded pieces of paper, cut from the exact middle of the fold up to the top edge of the square.

4. and **5.** Slide the flap marked 'x' through the paper doubled at 'o.'

6. Pull flap 'x' through and—gently!—hook it over the unused flap on the left-hand half of the heart. The other flap is now hooked over the flap marked 'o' and slid between the parts of the second flap on the left-hand half of the heart.

7. The heart is now finished, and should be fitted with a paper handle, using tape or glue.

8. to **10.** A slightly more complicated heart can be made by cutting twice in from the fold, an equal distance apart. First you weave one flap: hook over, then in between, then hook over. For the second: in between, hook over, in between. The third flap is woven in the same way as the first.

11. to **15.** Vary the appearance by making 4 to 6 flaps or try a wide central flap and two narrow outer flaps.

COOKIES AS ORNAMENTS

Dough ornaments made using cookie cutter shapes—or shaped by hand—captivate young and old in equal measure. Ornaments that follow a recipe replicating children's play-dough will last forever if lacquered with a dashing coat of paint or shellac—but, of course, no one should attempt to ingest these. Ginger or sugar doughs, understandably less durable, are meant to be munched; how can anyone resist plucking such deliciousness from the tree? And, of course, the edible versions are particularly enticing because of the immediate hope for a reward, be it a lick of the spoon or a nibble into a toasty, fresh-from-the-oven creation. If you do not own all the cookie cutter shapes you need, you can make your own templates from stiff cardboard; just draw the shape you want and cut it out and then cut around it onto your rolled-out dough as with a tracing.

An *enormous tree set up in a great room in a three-year-old saltbox in central Pennsylvania, above right, was rigged out with dozens of dragée-studded icing-coated wreaths. The silver dragées sparkle in the light cast by electric candles, above left. Red ribbons, tied into bows, match the thinner satin thread that was used to tie each wreath to its allocated branch, and the uniform effect of the combined decorations is, quite simply, delectable.*

A homemade, Scandinavian-inspired wood tree, "planted" in an old milk bucket, dances with smiling gingerbread men, above. Bright red ribbons and Red Delicious apples make the tree even livelier. Next to the candlestick, homemade blocks, milk-painted and letter-stenciled, proclaim the season.

Displaying the country virtues of simplicity and modesty, a fluffy pine tree, right, is dressed in crabapples and gingerbread hearts. Three wonderful fragrances—pine, apple, and gingerbread—combine to fill the common room with a unique, heady perfume.

COOKIE ORNAMENTS TO BAKE

A baker's kitchen in the weeks before Christmas is a hectic place, filled with enticing pies, cakes, and above all, cookies, cookies, and more cookies. Using her red gingham curtains as a backdrop, above, one baker has filled the kitchen windows with gingerbread men and hearts, and even given them their own tree on a side table.

Records show that Christmas trees were brought into homes in the German areas of Pennsylvania as early as the 1820s. These early trees were decorated with fruits, cookies, and toys. Nonedible cookies were sometimes made of salt and flour dough and saved from year to year. Our edible cookies are made for holiday enjoyment, as well as decoration.

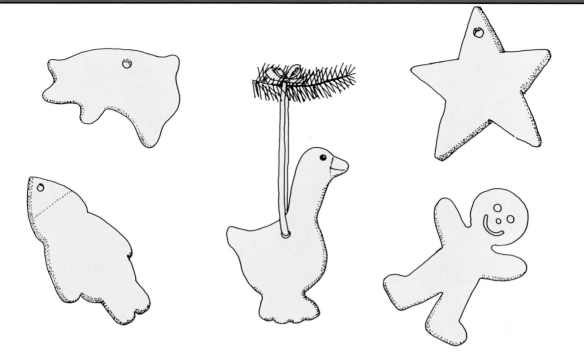

GINGERBREAD DOUGH

MAKES ABOUT 2 DOZEN COOKIES,
DEPENDING ON SIZE
5 cups unsifted all-purpose flour
2 teaspoons ground cinnamon
2 teaspoons ground ginger
½ teaspoon ground cloves
¼ teaspoon salt
1 cup vegetable shortening
¾ cup sugar
1 cup light molasses
1 large egg

1. On waxed paper, combine flour, cinnamon, ginger, cloves, and salt.

2. In large bowl, with electric mixer, beat shortening and sugar until light and fluffy. Beat in molasses and egg. Stir in flour mixture to make a stiff dough.

3. Heat oven to 350°F. Roll out dough to ⅛-inch thickness. Cut out cookies and transfer to ungreased baking sheet. With a toothpick, press a hole for ribbon in the top center of each cookie.

4. Bake gingerbread 12 to 15 minutes or until firm and golden brown. Cool cookies on wire rack.

SUGAR DOUGH

MAKES 4 DOZEN COOKIES

1 cup butter, softened
1 cup sugar
3 eggs, beaten
⅓ cup brandy
1 teaspoon mace
4 cups flour
Colored sugar, raisins, dragees, sprinkles
for decoration

1. Cream butter and sugar. Beat in eggs, brandy, and mace. Add sifted flour and work dough until smooth. Shape into a roll, wrap in plastic wrap or foil, and chill thoroughly.

2. Working on a lightly floured surface, roll dough out to 1/16-inch thickness and cut into desired shapes with cookie cutters. Place cookies on an ungreased baking sheet and sprinkle with colored sugar or other decoration. Use a toothpick to make a hole near the top of the cookie for inserting string after baking.

3. Bake at 375°F until golden, 8 to 9 minutes. Remove from sheet and cool on wire racks.

THE GIFTS OF CHRISTMAS

THE ART OF GIVING

A tender gesture, a kindness, a smile, a word, a happy thought, and a wrapped present are all joyful expressions of the art and act of giving. At Christmas, we open our hearts to family and friends with appreciation and undiluted delight. This is the time of year, too, though, when we should take the time and make the effort to give to those less fortunate than ourselves; food and clothing and toys are all gifts which are welcomed warmly by hospitals and churches. At home, every room becomes a gift, extending pleasure to all who gather to share in the greatest gift of all, which is this splendid season itself. But the season need not quit here; prolong goodwill into the rest of the year as a gift to yourself as well as to those around you.

Rearranged to attract everyone to the empathetic embrace of the fire, a cozy living room, above, focuses attention on gifts and gift-giving. Stockings hang from the mantel and beribboned boxes nestle under the tree. A hand-decorated bottle of Champagne stands at the ready with a medley of glass flutes to usher in the action.

An assortment of
unwrapped presents, above,
so beautiful that not one
needed further adornment,
was composed into a
sophisticated still-life upon a
table in front of the

Christmas tree. The collection
attests to the way in which
presentation can draw on
one's imagination as much as
the choice of the gift itself.

EARLY AMERICAN TOYS

If the heart and soul of Christmas resides in generosity and a spirit of giving, then a toy—more than any other gift, except perhaps for food—must reign as the quintessential offering. It goes without saying that toys appeal to children, but few grown-ups can resist a toy either. The well-chosen toy perfectly sums up feelings of affection and exemplifies a keen familiarity with and sense of caring for the recipient. For many adults, too, nostalgia for childhood seems to require an annual reaffirmation of meaning through remembrance, and favorite old toys such as a childhood doll or teddy are therefore brought proudly forward to take their rightful place among the holiday decorations. Collections of beloved antique toys happily mingle with wrapped gifts under the tree, stride or sprawl upon the mantel, highlight a bounty-laden table, or even, tread by tread, lead on up the stairs. Although toys now seem an integral part of Christmas, it was not until the Victorian times that they were bought specifically for play; early colonists

derided toys as sinful, and later, relenting somewhat, tolerated them, but only as miniature means of education. Many early toys were simply scaled-down versions of adult tools, or, like blocks, taught "learning" through game playing. Tops, balls, dolls, drums, and trains finally set precedents for gifts for play rather than merely for learning, or for cuddling and hugging and comfort.

One of the oldest games devised for children is blocks. Early blocks, cut and shaped by hand from wood remnants, were specifically decorated to be educational; many were embossed with letters of the alphabet to promote expertise in spelling and word construction. Later, blocks such as the kindergarten set from Hills, above, were papered on all six sides.

When the sides were set up correctly, the blocks formed a scene, sometimes embellished with a short quotation or poem or homily. During the latter part of the last century, picture blocks became a must for every child's stocking. Today block sets, in good condition, are a prime collectible.

A lone Santa, right, stands sentry among a glistening array of well-cared-for miniature farm tractors. Old and new machines attest to years of consistent manufacture. Names such as McCormick and John Deere would be advertised through these toy versions of their farm-sized equipment, and the models were designed both for play and, subliminally, to inspire parental preference for one name brand for real-life toil in the fields. A dollhouse, below right, would, in the same way, inculcate in a small consumer a knowledge of and appreciation for the Real Thing. A homemade dollhouse such as this one would offer years of play, too, because collecting miniatures — some store-bought and some lovingly crafted by hand at home — would inspire an ongoing involvement with the gift. A tiny cedar tree girdled with paper garlands and popcorn strings, below left, sets off one family's collection of antique toys. The collection includes a Noah's Ark populated by requisite two-by-twos, a patriotic Uncle Sam, and a tiny Raggedy Ann, as well as the always-mandatory teddies.

A miscellany of small toys, opposite, including a pair of easygoing jointless clowns, was collected in a bookcase in a farmhouse in Ohio and then interspersed with fresh greens. The clowns, as well as the polka-dotted tiger and the acrobat, were all manufactured by a Philadelphia toymaker, Schoenhut, in the early part of this century, and are prized collectibles. The paper-covered blocks display fragments of pictures, which, when stacked correctly, reveal sweet pictorial scenes and nursery rhymes.

Snuggled together on cozy rag rugs at the base of a diminutive evergreen, right, a coterie of porcelain-faced dolls awaits new arrivals; it is tempting to think that generous St. Nick might deposit some new toys among them to swell their ranks. The tree was hung with tiny ornaments suited to the scale of the scene.

Two Centuries of Santas

Born, so they say, as a god and translated into bishop then patron saint, the jolly old elf we know as Santa Claus has survived multiple personalities in his long career as gift-giver emeritus. He has his own saint's day, December 6, which was derived from the feast sponsored in his honor by Greeks and Romans to whom he was embodied in the form of Poseidon, god of the sea. The Nicholas of St. Nick was transplanted from Asia Minor to Europe, and there he assumed a variety of guises, dispensing his gifts on his own day, on Christmas Eve, on New Year's, or, emulating the Wise Men, on Epiphany, January 6. To Americans during the colonial era, gift-giving was considered extravagant and a sin; there was no Santa back then. It was the famous poem written by Clement C. Moore—*The Night Before Christmas*—and cartoon by Thomas Nast that crystallized the image of Santa Claus we love today. His name, extrapolated from the Dutch Sinterklass, stuck to the chubby septuagenarian, and collections of Santas are based upon this benevolent bearded fellow bearing gifts.

A curious card-and-string collaged Santa, opposite, hangs from a breadboard over the sink in a Minnesota kitchen; he is left there year-round to remind everyone of his perpetual faith in human kindness. He carries a small sprig of greenery as a gesture of hope and wears more greenery in his fur-trimmed cap.

Newly made "snickles and kringles," above, felt-and-batting re-creations of Belsnickles and Kris Kringles, cluster with a trio of celluloid reindeer dating from the 1930s. All feel right at home in a tidy forest of miniature snow-dusted trees, one of which is festively girdled with a string of red beads.

Enthusiastic Santa collectors hoard their St. Nicks by the score. The dozens assembled in a pie safe in Tennessee, above, step out to take their places around the cabin during the holidays. Antique Santas, both flat and rotund, center left, rest atop a brick mantelpiece in Minnesota. The clearest novelties are a bell with a baby-faced Santa head and a stubby Santa round of girth though small of head. Unusually garbed in non-traditional green, beige, white, and blue, a collection of antique and new Santas, below left, gathers with more conventionally attired counterparts against a backdrop of pewter plates.

Shortly after its publication 150 years ago, The Night Before Christmas spawned dozens of copiously illustrated hard- and paper-bound versions of its charming tale. Avid Santa lovers collected as many versions as possible, opposite right. And the Jolly Old Elf, initially depicted by Thomas Nast, soon took on a more expansive life, which was merrily featured in companion volumes. Santa, in other words, was no longer fettered to his December 24th ride through the sky, but was illustrated at work with his elves, relaxing by the fire with Mrs. Claus, and even taking vacations in the South.

THE TEDDY BEAR CELEBRATION

A country home usually can be counted on to have a few (or a great many) collectibles: an antique quilt, a set of spatterware, some handwoven baskets, perhaps a few hand-embroidered linens. At Christmas, though, one country collectible stands head-and-shoulders above the others. This is the teddy bear. Teddy bears seem to symbolize so much of the holiday's true spirit; they bring their characteristic sense of warmth, comfort, and humor to the season.

Many teddy bears were themselves once Christmas gifts, and displaying them for the holiday calls back memories of bygone celebrations, while giving a teddy bear begins a new tradition. With its wistful embroidered smile and trusting eyes, a teddy often presides over the festivities from a place of honor on the mantel or under the tree. A teddy may receive special holiday treatment: the rich caramel color of most bears goes well with berry-red and holly-green, and a special Christmas vest, muffler, or cap is entirely appropriate.

Set amid pine boughs in front of a beveled mirror, a venerable teddy bear, above, is surrounded by toys of his generation, including several tops and a rare Howdy Doody. Meanwhile, four teddies, opposite, in handknit sweaters and a tartan bowtie have been joined by a fashionable monkey on a horse-drawn carriage.

In an imaginative Christmas still-life, right, a teddy bear couple stand with a trio of Santas, some old wooden pins, a pair of wreaths, and a wedding portrait.

A pair of teddies are ready for their big moment as Christmas gifts, above, snuggled together in a wood bowl. For their journey they've brought along books and a candy cane as creature comforts.

Christmas hustle and bustle can take it out of the best of us, and sometimes a weary teddy, left, needs nothing so much as a little private time, an early night, and a favorite novel to dip into.

An exuberantly painted miniature piano, opposite, deriving its cavorting dancers from Botticelli and its cherubs from a Victorian Christmas card, was set up in front of an ornate cupboard to entice humans and chummy bears alike to revel in story and song. This orsine Stieff family—papa, mama, and baby bear—sports bright tartan bows, as well as their signature ear tags to mark the season and their illustrious Teutonic ancestry. The old storybook tells a wintry tale after caroling.

By the Chimney with Care

Two classic knit stockings, left, have been generously filled by Santa and topped off with three new teddies. Beyond the stockings, the rough-hewn mantel has been hung with delicate cranberry garlands and set with red heart-shaped candles.

Scraps of damaged patchwork quilts find new life as Christmas stockings, opposite. Even tiny bits of quilt can be cut into the familiar stocking shape and backed with cotton fabric. For longer life, quilt that is fragile should be lined before sewing. Completing the holiday scene, the family's collections of antique trees, Santas, and doggie doorstops are set out. Above all, an antique metal cow sports her own ribbon.

In the early nineteenth century, the tradition arose of hanging Christmas stockings from the mantel. The practice was inspired by the legend of St. Nick and his generosity toward the poor—which he demonstrated by filling their stockings with gold coins. At the outset, everyday socks and booties were hung by the fireplace. But the stockings soon took on more elaborate designs. Today, there is a rich range of stocking styles from the past to draw upon, from the patchwork pattern to richly embroidered designs. Homemakers might decorate such stockings with special needlework techniques or construct exuberant stockings from mismatched bits of fabric. Calico and plaid provide a rustic note, while appliquéwork allows for a rich range of figurative designs. You might recycle an old quilt to create a fireside stocking, and create matching pillow covers for sitting by the hearth. Or consider knitting patterned stockings in matched pairs. Romantic stockings can be made using springtime floral prints—a fresh and surprising counterpoint to sometimes too prevalently used Christmas red and green. Add eyelet ruffles and rickrack trim around the top of the stocking and thread a pretty satin ribbon along the top as a final flourish. Lace, in any width and in abundance, will make a stocking—even a hearty plaid one—graceful and feminine. For the toe of each stocking, drop in a tangerine or blood orange.

cold, sleety day provides
the time to get the presents
out of their hiding places.
Then I sit down for a quiet
wrapping session. My favorite
place for performing this
pleasant task is by the wood
stove. With a cup of tea
handy, it is delightful to
choose the paper and ribbon
for each box.

CHRISTMAS GIFT-WRAPPING

As a change of pace from commercially available wrappings, home-decorated paper, tie-ups, and tags show off ingenuity and spirit—and provide an opportunity for parents and children to get together to create unique and personalized packages.

Materials can be as simple as kraft paper, twine, and five-and-dime sticky stars or decals. Other papers to experiment with include shelf paper, newsprint or newspaper, and even untreated wallpaper, the kind that has no glue on the back. Plain paper is easy to decorate with freehand drawings or more controlled stencils.

To wrap overscaled or peculiarly shaped gifts, try fabric, which is not only pliable but also comes in wider widths than most papers. Small packages can be tied up with long shoelaces; yarn and embroidery floss and seam binding are alternatives to ribbon which can be picked up at the novelty counter in the dime store. Old Christmas cards can be recycled into gift tags by cutting out images or shapes from the front of the old card, then punching a hole into the shape so that it can be tied onto the gift.

Tiny tidy teddies, opposite, wearing their hearts as earnest expressions of their affection, were stenciled onto colorful wrapping paper in two stages—first the bears themselves and then their little valentine badges. The stencils, cut from a waxy paper available from the art supply store, match up, limb for limb, with their plush cousins. The twine used to tie up the gifts was first pulled through a paint-moistened sponge for a dash of color.

Presents potato-stenciled with stars and Santas cluster among a menagerie of antique toys under a Christmas tree, right, set up in front of a sunny window. Potatoes are easy for children to carve into stencils because the only tool necessary is a blunt knife. A butter knife best fits small fists. First cut the potato in half. If the stencil is to be long, like the Santa, cut the potato lengthwise and, conversely, if the shape is to be round or stubby, slice the potato across its width. Outline the shape with the tip of the knife and then scoop away from the demarcated silhouette to the outer edge of the potato. Dip the stencil into tempera paint set out in a flat dish. Blot once on paper toweling and then onto your paper.

Similar effects are achieved in two different ways, above: over solid-color wrapping paper, crocheted doilies have been gathered up and fastened with gold cord. A simple heart-shaped glass tree ornament and rose ribbon are the additional ornamentation. Another layered look is achieved by carefully cutting a pattern or a design such as the flower motif from tissue paper, which is wrapped over paper in a contrasting color. An artist's matte-knife is useful for intricate cutting such as this.

Childhood memories of Christmas feature intriguingly lumpy stockings and enormous glittering trees with sprawling piles of presents just waiting to be opened. Indeed, the act of opening a present captures in just those few seconds all the joy, the hope, and the great expectations of this day.

One classic look is achieved by wrapping all presents in paper and ribbon of the same color—all in white, or all in red—or to use white butcher's paper tied with gold cord. Paper doilies are fun for small presents, as are handkerchiefs either lacy or gingham. For last-minute giving, slip a few fresh-cut flowers or a decorative feather into the package bow. Dried cornhusks or a slender sheath of wheat are also homey decorations.

Some families traditionally give money or gift certificates to the children. These gifts can be hung on the tree, tucked inside handmade ornaments such as colorful felt sleighs or paper cornucopias or miniature stockings that are embroidered with the child's name and year.

Plain white bond paper, above, usually used for letters or for typing, was wrapped around a tiny box, and decorated with a green grid. Checkerboard squares were filled in with casual red-penciled scrawls. A sprig of holly with its berries perks up the pale-green gingham bow for added flair.

Handsome examples of wrapping with kraft paper, opposite, demonstrate how dressed up this paper can look. Larger packages have been painted with freehand water-color Santas; all are tied with tartan ribbon and are finished with clay pine trees and sprigs of real pine.

CHAPTER FIVE

THE
FOODS
OF
CHRISTMAS

SEASONAL GIFTS FROM THE KITCHEN
·
GIFTS OF FOOD
·
DESSERTS
·
BEVERAGES

Seasonal Gifts from the Kitchen

Gifts of food are true expressions of country spirit—the harvest of nature's bounty, lovingly prepared and generously offered. For with each gift of food, part of its maker is also given. Our first creature comfort, food nurtures and cossets and soothes us; as our first temptation, it excites and stimulates and enlivens us. And the pure pleasure to be had in preparing gifts of food is more than equalled by the appreciation of family and friends when they receive something made especially for them.

Many holiday festivities draw on food: carolers can defrost with mugs of steaming mulled cider and plates of gingerbread cookies; tree-trimming and gift-wrapping sessions are more fun when there are big bowls of spiced nuts to nibble on. Of all the traditional desserts, plum pudding with hard sauce is most popular for the Christmas dinner, especially when it is accompanied with a sparkling punch. But whatever food you choose to prepare and serve will not be of paramount importance. What matters most in holiday entertaining are the feelings, of togetherness and sharing, of tradition and renewal, of comfort and hope.

For many of us, the Christmas season is happily anticipated...then over in a flash. One good way to extend the Christmas feeling through the year is to extend your holiday cooking to other seasons. Though it seems that today almost any delicacy can be found on the shelves of super-markets and gourmet shops, the most interesting and memorable foods are those made at home. There is nothing like "homemade"—foods bursting with freshness and individuality (and totally lacking preservatives and additives). In the dog days of August, when you're surrounded by bushels of beefsteak tomatoes, shiny cucumbers, sweet peppers, and other garden abundance, put up a few jars of each to give in December.

Of course, Christmas gifts from your kitchen needn't be made only at the height of summer. Dense, moist fruitcakes will intensify their flavors when wrapped and set aside for as little as two weeks. Cookies and candies can be made in batches; pack up an assortment in a pretty box or tin lined with a paper doily—this is a special present!

In the following pages we've gathered some of our favorite recipes, recipes that we turn to year after year. We pass them along with the hope that you, too, will turn to them each holiday season.

A dessert table laden with old favorites and new treats, opposite, bespeaks the hospitality of Christmas. In place of a full cloth, a seasonal quilt runner runs along the middle of the tabletop. Firelight and candle glow, accents of pine, and a pot of hot chocolate complete the scene.

Creamy All-American Eggnog, above, recipe page 161

Peter & Nancy
love Susan

Jelly

Happy Holidays
Bob & Sandy

GIFTS OF FOOD

CRANBERRIES AND WALNUTS IN SHERRY

Photograph, opposite

This unusual condiment can be used with meat or game, or as a garnish for ice cream, or as an accompaniment to a cheese board.

MAKES TWO PINT JARS
1 cup water
1 pound (appproximately 4 cups)
  fresh cranberries, washed and
  picked over for stems
2½ cups sugar
Grated rind of 1 orange and 1 lemon
Juice of 1 orange and 1 lemon
1 cup chopped walnuts
½ cup dry sherry

1. Prepare two pint jars, lids, and bands for processing.
2. Bring water to boiling; add cranberries and simmer until the skins pop open.
3. Add sugar and grated orange and lemon rinds and their juices and simmer together 15 minutes.
4. Remove from heat; add walnuts and sherry, stirring well to combine.
5. Spoon into self-sealing sterilized jars. Fill to within ½ inch from top of jar. Process jars in boiling water bath for 15 minutes. Cool. Label jars and store in cool, dark, dry place.

Cranberries and Walnuts in Sherry
(center), recipe above

BOUNTIFUL BEAN SOUP MIX

Photograph, page 132

Colorful and easy to make, this gift is a good one for the kids to assemble. Ask them to print out the recipe to include with the mix.

MAKES ELEVEN 1-PINT JARS
1 pound dried red kidney beans
1 pound dried black beans
1 pound dried cow peas
1 pound dried chick peas
1 pound dried baby lima beans
1 pound red lentils
1 pound brown lentils
1 pound dried yellow split peas
1 pound dried green split peas
1 pound dried pinto beans

1. In large bowl, combine all ingredients until thoroughly mixed. Place in pint jars or bottles, seal and label.
2. Include the following instructions for bean soup: In 4-quart saucepan, heat 1 quart (4 cups) water and 2 cups bean soup mix to boiling over high heat. Boil 2 minutes. Cover pan; remove from heat; let beans soak 1 hour. Drain beans through large strainer. Wash saucepan and fry ¼ pound sliced bacon, chopped, over medium heat until crisp. Discard all but about 2 tablespoons fat. Add 1 carrot, peeled and chopped, and 1 clove garlic, finely chopped. Cook over medium-low heat until vegetables are soft. Add 6 cups water, 1 bay leaf; add drained bean mixture. Cover pan and heat to boiling over high heat. Reduce heat to low and simmer 1½ hours. Add salt and pepper to taste. Remove bay leaf before serving. Makes 8 cups of soup.

BACKWOODS RICE

Photograph, page 132

Dried fruits and nuts are common snacks in the woods; here they are added to a seasoned rice mixture. The recipe for preparing the rice should be given along with the mix. For a vegetarian dish, instant chicken-broth powder can be replaced with vegetable-broth powder.

MAKES FOUR 1⅓-CUP JARS
4 cups long-grain rice
½ cup dried apricots, finely chopped
½ cup dark seedless or golden
  raisins
½ cup walnuts, finely chopped
¼ teaspoon ground cinnamon
2 tablespoons instant chicken-broth
  powder
1 teaspoon dried orange peel
¼ teaspoon ground black pepper

1. In large bowl, combine all ingredients and mix well. Divide into four jars. Seal and label.
2. Be sure to include the following directions for cooking rice: In heavy 2-quart saucepan, heat 2 teaspoons vegetable oil and 1 teaspoon butter over medium-low heat. Add 1 medium-size onion, finely chopped, and sauté over medium heat until softened and just golden brown—2 to 5 minutes. Add 1 jar of Backwoods Rice and stir to coat with oil. Add 1¾ cups water. Heat mixture to boiling over high heat, stirring occasionally. Reduce heat to low; cover with tight-fitting lid. Simmer 15 to 20 minutes. Without uncovering, remove pot from heat and set aside in warm area 10 minutes; fluff rice with fork before serving.

FRESH HERB VINEGARS

The herb garden supplies fresh herbs for vinegars, which season home-grown vegetables, as well as meats, fish and poultry. You can virtually use any herb to make vinegar but the following are favorites: sweet basil, purple basil, thyme, tarragon, lovage, mint, sweet marjoram, bay laurel, rosemary, chive blossoms, dill, oregano, and salad burnett (tastes like cucumbers).

MAKES ABOUT 1 GALLON
1 gallon cider or white vinegar
Well-rinsed fresh herbs

(Top shelf from left to right) *Backwoods Rice*, recipe page 131; *Orange-Raisin Applesauce*, recipe page 133; *Creamy Mocha Fudge*, recipe page 139; (Lower shelf from left to right) *Mixed-Fruit Chutney*, recipe page 133; *Sweet Onion-Pepper Relish*, recipe page 133; *Bountiful Bean Soup Mix*, recipe page 131; *Sugar & Spice Nuts*, recipe page 138; (Bottom) *Eggnog Cakes*, recipe page 153

1. Pour off and reserve about half the contents of the vinegar jug.
2. Stuff the jug as full as possible with herbs. Top off the jug with some of the reserved vinegar; cover and place in the sun to steep for about 3 weeks or until vinegar is nicely flavored. Chive blossom vinegar should be placed in a brown paper bag and steeped in a dark place.
3. Funnel off vinegar into small bottles, placing a snippet of the fresh herb used in each bottle. Label bottles and store in cool, dark place.

ORANGE-RAISIN APPLESAUCE

Photograph, opposite

Zesty orange peel flavors this delightfully sweet applesauce. It makes a wonderful complement to roast duck and pork.

MAKES FOUR ½-PINT JARS
1 cup dark seedless raisins
¾ cup orange juice
1 tablespoon grated orange peel
1 24-ounce jar applesauce

1. Prepare four ½-pint jars and lids for processing.
2. In 2-quart saucepan, combine raisins, orange juice, and peel. Heat to boiling over medium heat. Stir in applesauce. Reheat to boiling, stirring often to prevent scorching.
3. Ladle sauce into drained, hot jars. Fill to within ½ from top of jar. Seal with lids and bands. Process in boiling water bath 10 minutes. Cool applesauce. Label jars and store in cool, dark, dry place.

SWEET ONION-PEPPER RELISH

Photograph, opposite

The availability of Spanish onions and sweet red peppers in markets in November and December make this relish practical as a Christmas gift. Refrigerated, it will keep for several weeks.

MAKES 5 CUPS
¼ cup vegetable oil
¾ cup sugar
2 large (1-pound each) sweet Spanish onions, peeled and sliced ¼ inch thick
2 large sweet red peppers, seeded and cut into ¼-inch strips
1 teaspoon salt or to taste
⅓ cup red-wine vinegar

1. Prepare five half-pint jars, lids, and bands for processing.
2. In large skillet, heat oil over medium-high heat just until it is very hot. Add sugar and heat until sugar turns caramel brown and dissolves completely, about 3 minutes.
3. Add onions, peppers, and salt. Reduce heat to medium. Cook, stirring frequently, until onions are soft and translucent—about 15 minutes.
4. Add vinegar. Cook over low heat 30 minutes. Remove from heat.
5. Spoon into self-sealing sterilized jars. Fill to within ½ inch from top of jar. Process jars in boiling water bath for 15 minutes. Cool. Label jars and store in cool, dark, dry place.

MARTHA'S PEPPERCORN MIX

Grind this colorful assortment of whole peppercorns through a peppermill. Instead of putting the mix in jars, give them away in glass or clear plastic mills.

MAKES FOUR ½-CUP JARS
2 1.87-ounce bottles black peppercorns (1 cup)
1 2.12-ounce bottle white peppercorns (½ cup)
1 0.5-ounce bottle freezed-dried green peppercorns (½ cup)
1 ounce dried pink or red peppercorns (½ cup)
½ cup whole allspice

In large bowl combine all ingredients and mix well. Divide into 4 glass jars. Seal and label jars.
Note: Freeze-dried green and pink peppercorns may be found in specialty food shops or may be mail-ordered from Paprikas-Weiss Co., 1546 Second Ave., New York, NY 10028.

MIXED-FRUIT CHUTNEY

Photograph, opposite

Tart yet spicy and sweet, this relish complements poultry or pork. Because it's made with canned fruit, it is particularly economical to make at Christmas.

MAKES ABOUT TWO 1-PINT JARS
1 29-ounce can cling peach halves
1 16-ounce can pear halves
½ cup sugar
¼ cup distilled white vinegar
1 large onion
1 clove garlic, finely chopped
¼ cup finely chopped crystallized ginger
½ teaspoon crushed red pepper
½ teaspoon salt
1 cup pitted prunes, each quartered

1. Prepare two 1-pint or four ½-pint jars, lids, and bands for processing.
2. Drain peaches and pears, reserving ¾ cup fruit syrup. In 4-quart saucepan, combine syrup, sugar, vinegar, onion, garlic, ginger, red pepper, and salt. Reduce heat to medium-low. Simmer 30 minutes, stirring occasionally. Taste mixture and add more sugar, if desired.
3. Meanwhile, cut drained fruit into 1-inch chunks. Stir fruit and prunes into onion mixture. Continue to cook until mixture is slightly thickened and translucent—about 30 minutes.
4. Spoon chutney into self-sealing sterilized jars. Fill to within ½ inch from top of jar. Process jars in boiling water bath for 10 minutes. Cool. Label jars and store in cool, dark, dry place.

A country house comes alive at Christmas, with family and friends dividing the time between the warmth of the living room fire and the tantalizing aromas of the kitchen, where Christmas dinner is well under way. Wearing baskets of greenery and garlands and wreaths, the house itself seems to glow.

PRETZELS

Photograph, page 148

Homemade soft pretzels were a popular item at Pennsylvania German Christmas fairs. The display in Winterhauers's Kershner Parlor, which inspired our picture, was an interpretation of such a fair held in December 1830 by the Dorcas Society of York, Pa.

MAKES 6 PRETZELS
5 cups unsifted all-purpose flour
1 package rapid-rising dry yeast
¾ teaspoon salt
1¼ cups very hot water (125° to 130° F)
Salt Dip (recipe follows)
Coarse salt

1. In large bowl, mix flour, yeast, salt, and hot water. Knead mixture in bowl until combined. Turn out onto a lightly floured board and knead until smooth. Form dough into ball. Invert bowl over dough and let rest 15 minutes.
2. Meanwhile, prepare Salt Dip. Grease 2 baking sheets with vegetable cooking spray or vegetable shortening. Divide dough into 6 pieces. On board, shape each piece into a 16-inch rope. Form each into a pretzel and dip in Salt Dip. Place pretzels on greased baking sheet. Sprinkle with coarse salt. Cover pretzels loosely with clean cloth and let rise in a warm place until double in size—about 30 minutes.
3. Heat oven to 400°F. Bake pretzels 15 to 20 minutes or until brown. These are best when eaten the day they are made.

SALT DIP
1 teaspoon salt
2 teaspoons baking soda
¾ cup water

Combine all ingredients in pie plate.

Cranberry-Nut Bread, recipe page 137

OLD-FASHIONED CRACKER BARREL CRACKERS

These are like the plain crackers that New England grocers used to sell loose from great old wood barrels. To recrisp them after storing, heat at 350°F for 5 to 7 minutes. They are delicious with cheese, preserves, and all by themselves.

MAKES ABOUT 40 CRACKERS
2 cups unsifted all-purpose flour
1 teaspoon salt
½ teaspoon baking powder
¼ cup (½ stick) butter or shortening
½ cup milk
1 large egg

1. Combine dry ingredients in a bowl and blend.
2. With a pastry blender or two knives, cut in butter until mixture resembles coarse meal.
3. Add milk and egg and mix to make a stiff dough.
4. Knead on a lightly floured board for about 5 minutes or until dough is smooth.
5. Divide dough in half. Set one part aside while rolling out the remainder. Heat oven to 400°F.
6. Roll dough out on a lightly floured board to about ⅛-inch thickness. Cut into rounds or desired shapes.
7. Place on lightly greased baking sheets. Prick crackers with a fork and bake about 10 minutes until lightly browned. Remove from racks. Crackers will crisp as they cool. Store cooled crackers in an airtight container.

CHEESE STICKS

Cheddar and blue cheese team up in these twisted pastry snacks. These are delicious, so if you're entertaining even a small group, you may want to double the recipe.

MAKES 18
2 cups unsifted all-purpose flour
½ cup (1 stick) butter or margarine, cut up
¼ pound Cheddar cheese, cut up
¼ pound blue cheese, crumbled
1 large egg yolk
1 teaspoon Worcestershire sauce
¼ teaspoon ground red pepper
Ground red pepper for topping

1. In container of food processor, with chopping blade, combine flour, butter, cheeses, egg yolk, Worcestershire sauce, and ¼ teaspoon red pepper. Process until well blended.
2. If mixing by hand, shred the Cheddar cheese first, then, in medium-size bowl, combine flour and red pepper. With pastry blender or 2 knives, cut butter and cheeses into flour mixture until mixture resembles coarse crumbs. Stir in Worcestershire sauce and egg yolk until well blended.
3. On lightly floured surface, pat dough into 6-inch square. Wrap and place in freezer for 30 minutes.
4. Roll dough out on floured surface to 18- by 8-inch rectangle. From short end, fold one third of dough over center third. Fold opposite one third over to make 8- by 6-inch rectangle. Repeat rolling and folding once more. Wrap in plastic wrap and place in freezer 30 minutes.
5. Heat oven to 350°F. Roll chilled dough into 13 ½- by 12-inch rectangles, about ⅛ to ¼ inch thick. Cut crosswise into eighteen ¾-inch-wide sticks. Sprinkle with red pepper. Place sticks, ½ inch apart, on ungreased baking sheets. Twist sticks; press ends lightly onto sheet.

6. Bake sticks 15 to 20 minutes, or until crisp and lightly browned. Remove sticks to wire rack to cool completely. Store in airtight containers.

CRANBERRY-NUT BREAD

Photograph, opposite

We bake these for giving in mini-loaf pans. For a large loaf, the batter can be baked in one 9- by 5- by 3-inch loaf pan. For freshness and sparkle, wrap the cooled breads in cellophane and tie with bright ribbons or gold cord.

MAKES 3 MINI-LOAVES OR 1 LARGER LOAF
1¾ cup unsifted all-purpose flour
½ teaspoon salt
½ teaspoon baking soda
1½ teaspoons baking powder
1 cup sugar
1 large egg
½ cup orange juice
¼ cup grated orange rind
¼ cup (½ stick) butter, melted
1 cup fresh cranberries, ground
½ cup chopped walnuts

1. Heat oven to 350°F. Butter three 5- by 3- by 2-inch loaf pans or one 9- by 5- by 3-inch pan.
2. Sift dry ingredients into bowl.
3. Beat egg with juice, rind, and butter; beat into flour mixture. Stir in cranberries and nuts.
4. Spoon batter into prepared pans and bake in center of oven 40 minutes for small loaves, 1 hour for the large one.
5. Cool 20 minutes. Turn out on a wire rack to complete cooling. Wrap and let stand overnight to improve flavor and allow easier slicing.

CHUNKY ZUCCHINI BREAD

Chunky Zucchini Bread is the perfect gift idea if you haven't had the time to start baking weeks ahead. It can even be given warm from the oven, although it will slice better if it has had a chance to stand overnight.

MAKES 2 LOAVES
3 cups unsifted all-purpose flour
1½ cups sugar
4½ teaspoons baking powder
1 teaspoon salt
½ teaspoon ground nutmeg
1½ cups chopped zucchini
1½ cups chopped walnuts
1 cup vegetable oil
4 large eggs
2 teaspoons grated lemon rind
Walnut halves (optional)

1. Heat oven to 350°F. Grease and flour two 8½- by 4½-inch loaf pans.
2. In large bowl, combine flour, sugar, baking powder, salt, and nutmeg. Stir in zucchini and walnuts. In a small bowl, combine oil, eggs, and lemon rind.
3. Stir liquid ingredients into flour mixture just until moistened. Spread batter evenly in prepared loaf pans. If desired, garnish with walnut halves.
4. Bake until toothpick inserted in center comes out clean, about 1 hour. Cool in pans on wire rack 10 mintues; remove from pans and cool completely. Store overnight tightly wrapped in plastic before slicing.

APPLE BUTTER

Traditionally, apple butter was cooked outside in large kettles over an open fire. Often, it was the occasion of a family get-together. Today it may be made on an electric stove, but it still has old-time integrity.

MAKES 4 CUPS
3 pounds tart apples
2 cups unfiltered apple cider
1 cup granulated sugar
¼ cup light-brown sugar
½ teaspoon ground cinnamon
¼ teaspoon ground cloves

1. Prepare four half-pint jars, lids, and bands for processing.
2. Peel and core apples; cut into eighths. In heavy 6-quart saucepot or Dutch oven, heat apples and cider to boiling. Simmer 20 minutes or until apples are very soft.
3. Stir mixture with fork, breaking up apples, to make sauce. Stir in sugars, cinnamon, and cloves. Cook, uncovered, over low heat, 1½ to 2 hours, or until desired consistency, stirring frequently.
4. Spoon into self-sealing sterilized jars. Fill to within ½ inch from top of jar. Process jars in boiling water bath for 10 minutes. Cool. Label jars and store in cool, dark, dry place.

AUNT SARAH'S LEMON CURD

Part of our English heritage, this tangy treat is growing more popular all the time. People who love lemon pie will adore lemon curd.

MAKES 3 CUPS
4 large eggs
Few grains of salt
1¾ cups sugar
¼ cup butter, at room temperature
2 tablespoons grated lemon peel
½ cup fresh lemon juice

1. Beat the eggs in the top of a double boiler.
2. Stir in remaining ingredients and cook over simmering water about 30 minutes, stirring frequently until thick and smooth. Lemon Curd will thicken more when cooled.
3. Cool, cover, and refrigerate. Spoon lemon curd into 1-cup crocks or jars, cover with plastic wrap and tie with ribbon. Keeps 2 to 3 weeks in refrigerator.

NUT BRITTLE

With this quick recipe you can make a distinctive gift in no time. A mixture of nuts with a few candied cherry halves makes a pretty variation.

MAKES 1½ POUNDS
2 cups sugar
2 cups chopped pecans or walnuts

1. Butter a baking sheet well. In a heavy skillet, melt sugar slowly until light golden brown.
2. Add nuts quickly; stir well. Turn out onto buttered baking sheet. Cool. Break into large pieces and store in a container with a tight-fitting lid.

SUGAR & SPICE NUTS

Photograph, page 132

Called Swedish nuts by some, mixed nuts are made in a large batch that can be divided to give as several gifts.

MAKES ABOUT 2 POUNDS
¾ cup (1½ sticks) butter or
  margarine
2 large egg whites, at room
  temperature
1 cup sugar
1 tablespoon ground cinnamon
½ teaspoon salt (if nuts are
  unsalted)
2 12-ounce cans mixed nuts or
  about 5 cups mixed almonds,
  walnuts, and pecans

1. Heat oven to 325°F. Line 15½- by 10½-inch jelly-roll pan with heavy-duty aluminum foil. Place butter in lined pan; melt in oven while oven is heating.
2. In large bowl, with electric mixer at high speed, beat egg whites until foamy. Gradually beat in sugar until stiff peaks form. Beat in cinnamon and salt, if using. With rubber spatula, fold in nuts.
3. Spread nut mixture over melted butter in pan. Bake 30 minutes, stirring 3 or 4 times to keep nuts separated during baking. Cool nuts in pan on wire rack 5 minutes. With slotted spoon or pancake turner, transfer nuts to brown-paper- or waxed-paper-lined tray or pan to cool completely. Store nuts in jars or tightly covered containers.

CREAMY MOCHA FUDGE

Photograph, page 132

Coffee and coffee liqueur add dimension to a rich chocolate walnut fudge; the recipe is easy and quick, and can be made up to a couple hours ahead.

MAKES 2½ POUNDS OR 16 PIECES
1 ⅓ cups sugar
⅔ cup evaporated milk
1 7- or 8-ounce jar marshmallow creme
¼ cup (½ stick) butter
¼ cup Kahlúa, Tia Maria, or other coffee liqueur
2 tablespoons instant-coffee powder or granules
1 12-ounce package semisweet chocolate chips
1 cup chopped walnuts
1 teaspoon vanilla extract

1. Line 8-inch square baking pan with aluminum foil; set aside.
2. In 2-quart saucepan, combine sugar, milk, marshmallow creme, butter, coffee liqueur, and instant coffee. Heat to boiling over medium-high heat, stirring constantly. Boil 5 minutes.
3. Remove from heat; stir in chocolate chips until melted. Stir in nuts and vanilla. Spread fudge into prepared pan. Refrigerate until firm.
4. Remove fudge from pan and discard foil. Cut fudge into squares. Wrap in plastic wrap and tie with ribbons.

CHOCOLATE-DIPPED STRAWBERRIES

Delicious, elegant, impressive, and foolproof—what more can one ask from a Christmas gift? Though expensive in specialty stores, chocolate-dipped berries and other fruits are a snap to make at home.

MAKES 2 DOZEN BERRIES
2 dozen large unblemished (preferably tart) strawberries, caps left on
2 ounces (2 squares) semisweet chocolate, melted according to package directions

1. Cover baking sheet or tray with aluminum foil or waxed paper. Wash berries quickly in cool running water or brush them with a damp pastry brush to clean. Dry gently but thoroughly.
2. Stir chocolate until smooth. Holding berries by the cap end, dip one at a time into the chocolate, coating about two thirds of the way up the berry. Scrape excess chocolate from the tip on the edge of the pan. Place berries on baking sheet as coated.
3. When all berries are dipped, refrigerate for at least 15 minutes to harden the chocolate. Berries will keep in the refrigerator for 24 hours. Serve on a platter with other fruits or with a decorative nosegay of violets.
Note: Fresh pineapple segments, seedless green grapes, and tangerine segments also lend themselves to this treatment.

CHOCOLATE-DIPPED CRYSTALLIZED GINGER

Some might say this is gilding the lily, but the combination of these two unique flavors makes a memorable sweet candy.

MAKES ¾ POUND
4 1-ounce squares semisweet chocolate
½ pound crystallized ginger pieces

1. In the top of a double boiler, over hot but not boiling water, melt chocolate.
2. Spread foil or waxed paper on a baking sheet. Dip each piece of ginger into chocolate to cover half of it. Allow excess to drip back into double boiler. Place on baking sheet.
3. When all ginger has been dipped, place baking sheet in refrigerator until chocolate is firm. Remove candy from waxed paper and stack between layers of waxed paper in an airtight container. Refrigerate until ready to serve.

Lemon Spritz Cups, recipe below

LEMON SPRITZ CUPS

Piping these cookies through a pastry bag gives them a pretty, uniform look.

MAKES ABOUT 9 DOZEN
1 cup (2 sticks) butter or margarine, softened
1 3-ounce package cream cheese, softened
⅔ cup sugar
2 large eggs
2½ cups unsifted all-purpose flour
1 teaspoon baking powder
½ teaspoon lemon extract
1 tablespoon finely grated lemon rind
1 tablespoon lemon juice
Candied green cherries, cut into ¼-inch pieces for garnish

1. In large bowl, with electric mixer, beat butter and cream cheese until fluffy. Beat in sugar and eggs until well mixed. Stir in 1 cup flour, the baking powder, and lemon extract, rind, and juice. With spoon, stir in remaining flour (about 1½ cups) until dough is smooth and fluffy.
2. Heat oven to 375°F. Line miniature muffin pans with 1-inch fluted paper cups or use foil-and-paper cups placed on baking sheet. Spoon a small amount of cookie dough into pastry bag fitted with large star or rosette tip. Pipe swirls of dough to fill each paper cup. Garnish center of each wih a piece of cherry. Continue with remaining dough.
3. Bake 20 minutes or until golden. Remove from pans; cool on wire racks. Repeat with remaining dough. Store in airtight container.

PISTACHIO BROWNIES

Besides being moist and chocolaty, these brownies are a cinch to make: All the mixing is done in one pan!

MAKES 4 DOZEN
1 cup (2 sticks) butter or margarine
4 1-ounce squares unsweetened chocolate
1½ cups sugar
3 large eggs
2 teaspoons vanilla extract
1 cup unsifted all-purpose flour
¼ teaspoon baking powder
½ cup chopped unsalted pistachios
Chocolate Glaze (recipe follows)
Finely chopped unsalted pistachios

1. Lightly grease and flour a 13- by 9-inch baking pan. Heat oven to 325°F.
2. In 2-quart saucepan, melt butter and chocolate over low heat, stirring constantly with wooden spoon. Remove from heat; stir in sugar until well mixed. Stir in eggs and vanilla until blended.
3. Stir flour and baking powder into chocolate mixture until well blended. Stir in ½ cup pistachios. Pour batter into prepared pan, spreading evenly.
4. Bake 35 to 40 minutes or until edges start to pull away from side of pan. Cool brownies completely in pan on wire rack. Cut brownies lengthwise into 4 strips; then cut each strip crosswise into 12 bars.
5. Prepare Chocolate Glaze. Remove brownies, one at a time, from pan. With small metal spatula spread chocolate over top and sides until coated. Place brownies, about 1 inch apart, on wire racks over waxed paper to dry. Scrape chocolate drippings off waxed paper and

Pistachio Brownies, recipe left

reheat to use if necessary. Sprinkle bars with finely chopped pistachios. Place each glazed brownie in a fluted cup. Store in single layer on a tray in refrigerator.

CHOCOLATE GLAZE

MAKES ABOUT 1¼ CUPS
½ cup unsweetened cocoa powder
¾ cup sugar
¼ cup (½ stick) unsalted butter (do not use margarine)
½ cup heavy cream
Pinch of salt
½ teaspoon vanilla extract

In 1-quart heavy saucepan, mix all ingredients except vanilla. Cook over medium heat to dissolve sugar, stirring ocassionally. Heat to boiling, stirring often; boil 2 minutes. Remove from heat; cool to room temperature. Stir in vanilla.

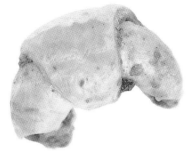

Raisin-and-Pecan Crescents, recipe below

RAISIN-AND-PECAN CRESCENTS

Cream cheese makes a rich yet flaky pastry, which we fill with sweetened pecans and raisins.

MAKES 5 DOZEN

2 cups unsifted all-purpose flour
½ cup (1 stick) butter or margarine
1 8-ounce package cream cheese
2 large eggs
2 tablespoons water

Filling:

1 cup finely chopped pecans
⅔ cup sugar
½ cup dark seedless raisins, finely
 chopped
1 tablespoon ground cinnamon

1. In large bowl, place flour. With pastry blender or 2 knives, cut in butter and cream cheese until mixture resembles coarse crumbs. In cup, beat eggs and water with fork. Stir about half the egg mixture into flour mixture until dough begins to hold together. (Reserve remaining egg mixture for glaze.) With hands, press mixture into mound; divide into 6 balls. Wrap each with plastic; refrigerate dough until firm enough to handle—about 1 hour.
2. Heat oven to 350°F. Grease 2 large baking sheets. Prepare filling: In small bowl, combine ingredients.

3. On floured surface, roll one ball of dough into a 9-inch circle; brush lightly with reserved egg mixture; sprinkle about ⅓ cup filling in a thin layer over dough. Cut dough into 10 wedges.
4. From the curved edge, roll up each wedge to the point. Place wedges point-side down about 1 inch apart, on greased baking sheet. Bend the ends to curve into a crescent shape. Repeat with other pieces of dough.
5. Brush each crescent lightly with egg mixture. Bake 20 to 25 minutes or until golden brown. Cool crescents on wire racks. Store in airtight container with waxed paper between layers.

MOLDED SHORTBREAD COOKIES

This is the time to use those shortbread molds someone gave you last Christmas or try out some old molds you have been using for decoration. Even a well-seasoned cornstick pan can make interesting, if unorthodox, shortbreads. Shortbread is surely one of the simplest and most miraculous of cookies, with spectacularly delicious results from little effort and few ingredients. If you do not have a mold, try baking the shortbread in a scalloped quiche pan, marking the dough off with a fork before baking to form the classic wedge-shaped portions.

MAKES 1 8-INCH ROUND MOLD
 OR 3 BREADS IN A CAST-IRON
 CHANTICLEER MOLD

1 cup butter (2 sticks) at room
 temperature
¾ cup confectioners' sugar
1½ cups all-purpose flour
¼ cup corn starch
⅛ teaspoon salt

1. Heat oven to 325°F. Grease a seasoned shortbread mold. Wipe out excess oil. If mold is very complex, spray-on vegetable shortening is easier.
2. Beat the butter and sugar together until well mixed and slightly fluffy.
3. Work in flour, cornstrach, and salt with hands until mixture holds together and is smooth.
4. Spread mixture into mold and press in firmly. Bake about 45 minutes until light brown and still just slightly springy in the middle. Cooking times will vary depending on the composition of the mold. Turn shortbread out onto a wire rack and cool.

LEMON SHORTBREAD: Work 2 teaspoons finely grated lemon peel into the dough.

GINGERED SHORTBREAD: Add ½ teaspoon ground ginger or 1 tablespoon finely chopped crystallized ginger.

ALMOND LOAVES

Almond loaves are one of our favorite cookies: They look like little French baguettes and they're super-easy to make.

MAKES 32
1 cup whole blanched almonds
2 cups unsifted all-purpose flour
½ cup (1 stick) butter or margarine, softened
¾ cup sugar
1 teaspoon almond extract
¼ teaspoon salt
¼ teaspoon baking powder
3 large egg whites
Ground mace or nutmeg

1. In blender at medium speed or in food processor, blend or process almonds until very finely ground. (You should have about 1⅓ cups.)
2. In large bowl, combine flour and remaining ingredients except 1 egg white and mace. With electric mixer at low speed, beat until blended, occasionally scraping the bowl with rubber spatula. Stir in ground almonds. With hands, knead mixture into ball.
3. Heat oven to 350°F. Grease large baking sheet. Divide dough into 32 balls. Form each into 2½- by ¾-inch loaf. Place loaves 1 inch apart on greased baking sheet. Slash top of each 3 times. Brush loaves with reserved egg white; lightly sprinkle with mace.
4. Bake loaves 15 to 20 minutes or until golden brown. Cool on wire racks. Store in airtight container.

Strawberry Bonbons, recipe below

STRAWBERRY BONBONS

Colorful and fun, our bonbons are sweet sugar cookies with surprise secret centers of almonds or apricots, covered with strawberry-flavored icing, and decorated with sesame seeds and green frosting leaves to look like the real berry. The cookies may be baked ahead but should not be iced more than several hours before gift-giving.

MAKES 2 DOZEN
½ cup (1 stick) butter or margarine, softened
¾ cup confectioners' sugar
1 tablespoon vanilla extract
1½ cups unsifted all-purpose flour
1 to 2 tablespoons milk (optional)
About 24 whole blanched almonds, toasted, or 12 dried apricots, each cut in half
Strawberry Icing (recipe follows)
1 tablespoon sesame seeds, toasted
Royal Frosting (recipe, page 143)

1. In large bowl, with electric mixer, beat butter, sugar, and vanilla until fluffy. At low speed, beat in flour until well mixed. If dough is too dry to form a ball, add milk.

2. Heat oven to 350°F. Divide dough into 24 equal pieces. Wrap a piece of dough around an almond or folded apricot half; shape into a strawberry. Place cookies, about 1 inch apart, on ungreased baking sheet.
3. Bake 15 to 20 minutes or until set but not brown. Cool cookies on wire rack.
4. Prepare Strawberry Icing. Dip cookies, one at a time, in icing, letting excess drip back into bowl. As each cookie is dipped, place, round-side up, on wire rack over waxed paper. (It may be necessary to spread icing on dipped cookies with a small spatula to completely cover cookie.) Immediately sprinkle each lightly with sesame seeds before icing sets.
5. When cookies are dry, place in small fluted paper cups. Prepare Royal Frosting. Tint one fourth of frosting (¼ cup) green with food coloring. Spoon into small decorating bag fitted with a leaf tip. Pipe leaves onto wider top edge of each strawberry bonbon. Let leaves dry before packing. Store in single layer in airtight container at room temperature.

STRAWBERRY ICING

¼ cup strawberry jelly
2 tablespoons lemon juice
2 ½ cups sifted confectioners' sugar
⅛ teaspoon salt
Red food coloring
1 to 2 teaspoons water

In 1-quart saucepan, heat jelly and lemon juice over low heat until melted and smooth. Remove from heat. Stir in confectioners' sugar and salt until smooth. Add several drops food coloring to tint deep pink. Add enough water to thin icing to spreading consistency, if necessary.

Almond Loaves, recipe above

Mint Meringue Wreaths, recipe below

MINT MERINGUE WREATHS

When strung with ribbon, these light and airy wreaths also make great ornaments for your kitchen or dining room Christmas tree.

MAKES 3 TO 3½ DOZEN
4 large egg whites, at room
    temperature
½ teaspoon cream of tartar
1 cup sugar
½ teaspoon mint extract
Green food coloring
Royal Frosting (recipe follows)

1. In large bowl, with electric mixer, beat egg whites and cream of tartar until soft peaks form. Beat in sugar, 2 tablespoons at a time, until stiff, glossy peaks form.
2. Beat in mint extract and then enough food coloring to tint green. Spoon some meringue into pastry bag fitted with large star or rosette tip. Keep remaining meringue covered with plastic wrap.
3. Heat oven to 200°F. Line 3 large baking sheets with brown paper or aluminum foil. Trace twelve to fifteen 2½-inch circles, about 1 inch

apart, on the paper or foil. Pipe meringue decoratively within the circles into wreaths, leaving about 1- to 1¼-inch opening for the center of the wreath.
4. Bake meringues 1½ to 2 hours or until firm and dry but not brown. Turn off oven to cool. Carefully peel wreaths from paper or foil.
5. Prepare Royal Frosting. Tint about one third of frosting (⅓ cup) red with food coloring. Spoon into waxed-paper cone fitted with small writing tip. Pipe small dots on wreaths to resemble berries. Let frosting dry; store wreaths in airtight container.

ROYAL FROSTING

MAKES ABOUT 1 CUP
1 large egg white, at room
    temperature
¼ teaspoon cream of tartar
2¼ to 2½ cups sifted confectioners'
    sugar
Food coloring (optional)

In small bowl, with electric mixer at high speed, beat egg white with cream of tartar until foamy. Gradually beat in confectioners' sugar until frosting stands in stiff peaks and will hold its shape when dropped from a spoon. Leave frosting white or tint with food coloring as in cookie recipe. Cover surface of frosting directly with plastic wrap to prevent a crust forming.

APRICOT CORNUCOPIAS

Photograph, page 146

As a symbol of abundance, the cornucopia is especially appropriate for a country Christmas celebration. Our cornucopia-shaped cookies are filled with tangy apricot preserves.

MAKES 3 DOZEN
2½ cups sifted cake flour
⅓ cup sugar
⅓ cup vegetable oil
1 teaspoon baking powder
½ teaspoon salt
1 tablespoon grated lemon rind
2 large eggs
½ cup apricot preserves
1 large egg yolk
2 teaspoons cold water

1. Combine flour, sugar, oil, baking powder, salt, rind, and eggs in large bowl; mix well. Gather dough in ball; sprinkle with flour. Wrap in wax paper. Chill 1 hour or until dough is firm enough to handle.
2. Heat oven to 350°F. Divide dough in half. Roll one-half (keep other half chilled) on floured surface to ⅛-inch thickness. Cut into circles with floured 3-inch scalloped cookie cutter. Place circles, about ½ inch apart, on aluminum foil-lined baking sheets.
3. Spoon about ½ teaspoon preserves into center of circle; spread toward one edge. Bring one third of circle over preserves, leaving edge exposed. Bring other third of circle over first fold to form cornucopia.
4. Beat yolk and water in bowl; brush each cornucopia. Bake until golden—about 15 minutes. Transfer to wire rack with broad spatula. Cool. Reroll trimmings and repeat with other half of dough.

GINGERBREAD "REDWARE" COOKIES

Firm and brittle, these gingerbread cookies resemble real old-time redware pottery. Use the frosting to add holiday greetings to the standard "squiggle" design.

MAKES 32

½ cup (1 stick) buttter or margarine
1 cup dark corn syrup
¾ cup firmly packed dark-brown
  sugar
4¼ to 4½ cups unsifted all-purpose
  flour
1 tablespoon ground cinnamon
2 teaspoons ground ginger
2 teaspoons ground cloves
3 large eggs
2 tablespoons water
Royal Frosting (see Mint Meringue
  Wreaths recipe)

1. In 1-quart saucepan, melt butter over low heat; stir in corn syrup and brown sugar until well mixed. Remove from heat.
2. In large bowl, with electric mixer at low speed, beat butter mixture, 2 cups flour, the cinnamon, ginger, and cloves until well mixed. With spoon, stir in remaining flour until very stiff dough forms. (Dough should be firm enough to form a slightly sticky ball.) You may have to knead the last of the flour into dough until a ball forms.

3. Divide dough in half; wrap with plastic wrap, shaping each into a 3-inch-diameter cylinder. Refrigerate several hours or overnight.
4. Heat oven to 350°F. Invert six or more 3½-inch fluted round tart pans or 6-ounce custard cups and place on jelly-roll pan for ease in handling. (The tart-pan bottom should be about 2½ inches in diameter.) Grease the outside bottom of each tart pan. Unwrap and cut one dough cylinder into 16 slices. With lightly floured fingers, shape each dough slice into a perfect 3-inch round; press onto greased tart-pan bottom to cover and extend ¼ inch down and around the side.
5. Bake cookies 25 minutes or just until firm and top springs back when lightly pressed with fingertip. Meanwhile, separate 2 eggs, placing whites in a small bowl and yolks in a cup. (Use one of the egg whites for the Royal Frosting, if desired, and use other egg white in another recipe.) Beat remaining egg and water into yolks.
6. Remove jelly-roll pan from oven; place on wire rack to cool cookies a minute. Remove cookies from tart pans. Turn cookies over onto ungreased baking sheet. (The top of cookie is now the bottom of the "plate.") Brush cookies generously on the inside with some egg mix-

ture. Return cookies to oven; bake 10 minutes longer or until glazed and reddish brown.
7. Cool cookies on wire rack. Repeat to bake all dough slices. (If you have more tart pans or custard cups, you will be able to bake these cookies faster.) Store cookies in airtight containers if made ahead. (Be sure to refrigerate reserved egg white for the frosting if not decorating cookies right away.)
8. To decorate cookies: Prepare Royal Frosting. Tint half of the frosting (½ cup) yellow with food coloring. Spoon into decorating bag fitted with small writing tip. Pipe frosting onto cookies to decorate. Let frosting dry; store decorated cookies in a single layer on a tray, covered with waxed paper.

Gingerbread "Redware" Cookies, recipe above

CHRISTMAS ESSENCE

*Chop the peels of ½ a large orange and ½ a large lemon.
Mix with 1 large stick of cinnamon broken into bits, 6 whole cloves
and 2 large bay leaves. Wrap in a brightly colored square of cloth or tiny
tin; label. To use, simmer mixture in 2 cups of water
to create a spicy scent all through the house.*

WHITE CHOCOLATE NUGGETS

Make these chewy fruit cookies several weeks ahead to allow the flavors to mellow and the cookies to soften. Then drape them in sleek white chocolate.

MAKES 56

1 cup honey
⅔ cup firmly packed light-brown sugar
1 large egg
2 teaspoons grated lemon rind
1 tablespoon lemon juice
3 cups unsifted all-purpose flour
1 teaspoon ground cinnamon
1 teaspoon cloves
½ teaspoon ground nutmeg
½ teaspoon baking soda
¼ teaspoon salt
1 cup finely chopped walnuts
1 11-ounce container diced dried fruit mix
1¼ pounds white chocolate, finely chopped
¼ cup vegetable shortening

1. In 1-quart saucepan, heat honey over medium heat to boiling; remove from heat and cool.

White Chocolate Nuggets, recipe above

2. In large bowl, with electric mixer, beat sugar and egg until smooth and fluffy. At low speed, beat in lemon rind and juice, 1 cup flour, the spices, baking soda, and salt until well mixed.
3. With wooden spoon, stir in nuts and dried fruit. Stir in remaining flour until a stiff dough forms, kneading in flour at the end. Dough should be soft but workable.
4. Wrap dough with plastic wrap; refrigerate several hours or overnight. (Dough will be sticky but manageable to shape.)
5. Heat oven to 375°F. Lightly grease 1 large or 2 small baking sheets. Cut the dough into 4 equal pieces. On lightly floured board or cloth, shape each piece into a cylinder about 14½ inches long and 1 inch in diameter. Place, about 2 inches apart, on greased baking sheets. (If using small baking sheets, only bake 2 on a sheet because dough will spread.) Using flat metal spatula and your fingers, shape the ends of each cylinder into a diagonal (in opposite direction of each other.)
6. Bake 20 to 25 minutes or until golden brown. Cool on wire racks. Wrap cylinders in aluminum foil; place in plastic bags; store at room temperature at least 2 weeks before coating.
7. To cut each cylinder, using a ruler as a guide, cut first cookie diagonally opposite from the diagonal of the end piece, so that cookie measures about 1½ inches on widest side by ½ inch on narrowest side. Make second cookie cut on same diagonal

direction as the end piece. Alternate diagonal direction cuts along entire cylinder or log. You should end up with a total of 14 semi-pointed pieces per log.
8. In double boiler over hot, not boiling water (water temperature should be 120°F), melt half the finely chopped white chocolate and all of the shortening until smooth. Gradually stir in remaining chocolate. Remove pan from water; replace water in bottom of pan with warm (95°F) water. Place pan of chocolate back over warm water. Cool chocolate, stirring constantly, to 95°F.
9. Pour half of chocolate into medium-size bowl. (Keep other half warm over water.) Stir and cool to 80°F. Add a spoonful of 95°F chocolate; stir and add small amounts to bring temperature to 83° to 88°F for dipping. Dip each cookie into chocolate, coating all sides. Let as much drip off back into bowl as possible before placing on wire rack over waxed paper. (As needed, add 95°F chocolate to bowl; stir and cool before using.) Let chocolate harden before removing cookies from rack. Place white chocolate nuggets in single layer airtight container at cool room temperature.

SUGAR COOKIES

The most versatile of all cookies and the one of the most enjoyed, sugar cookies can be dressed up with colored sugar, silver dragées, sprinkles, and colored frostings. Make them with round cookie cutters or use ones with Christmas shapes.

MAKES 40 2½-INCH COOKIES

2 cups unsifted all-purpose flour
1½ teaspoons baking powder
¼ teaspoon salt
½ cup (1 stick) butter, softened
¾ cup sugar
1 large egg
1 tablespooon vanilla extract
1 tablespoon milk
Colored sugar (optional)

1. On piece of waxed paper, sift together flour, baking powder, and salt. In large bowl, with electric mixer, beat butter and sugar until light and fluffy. Add egg, vanilla, and milk and beat until smooth.

2. Fold in dry ingredients to form stiff dough. Wrap in plastic and refrigerate 1 hour.

3. Heat oven to 375°F. Roll dough to ⅛-inch thickness on lightly floured surface. Cut out with 2½-inch cookie cutter and place on ungreased baking sheet. Sprinkle with colored sugar, if desired.

4. Bake 8 to 10 minutes or until golden on edges. Cool on wire racks and store in airtight container.

Pistachio-Almond Logs, recipe page 147; *Orange Bonbon Cookies*, recipe page 147; *Lemon Spritz Cups*, recipe page 140; and *Apricot Cornucopias*, recipe page 143

ORANGE BONBON COOKIES

Photograph, opposite

Years ago, these old-fashioned orange cookies used to be made only around the holidays, when oranges were widely available.

MAKES 4 DOZEN
1 cup (2 sticks) butter or margarine
½ cup confectioners' sugar
¼ teaspoon salt
½ teaspoon vanilla extract
2 to 2¼ cups unsifted all-purpose flour
1 tablespoon grated orange rind
1 16-ounce package confectioners' sugar, sifted
⅓ cup orange juice
1 teaspoon orange extract
2 drops red food coloring
6 drops yellow food coloring

1. Beat butter, ½ cup confectioners' sugar, salt, and vanilla in large bowl until light and fluffy. Stir in 2 cups flour and orange rind with spoon. Add enough remaining flour, if necessary, to make dough firm and not sticky to the touch. Shape dough into 6- by 8-inch rectangle; wrap in waxed paper. Chill dough 3 hours or freeze 30 minutes.
2. Heat oven to 400°F. Cut dough into 6 strips lengthwise; then cut across into 8 strips. Roll pieces of dough gently between palms of hands to form balls about 1 inch in diameter. Place about 1 inch apart on ungreased baking sheet. Bake until light golden—10 to 12 minutes. Transfer to wire racks with spatula; cool.
3. Combine 16 ounces sugar, orange juice, extract, and food colorings in bowl; beat until smooth. If icing is too thick for dipping cookies, add water, ½ teaspoon at a time, until icing is spoonable. Put cookies, about six at a time, in icing. Toss gently with fork until coated. Lift out

cookies and place, rounded side up, on wire rack over waxed paper or flat pan. Let excess icing drip onto paper or pan. If needed, scrape up icing and return to bowl to use, stirring until smooth. Let icing set before storing cookies.

Pretzel Cookies, recipe below

PRETZEL COOKIES

Everyone likes pretzels, and these sweet ones are no exception.

MAKES 40
¾ cup (1½ sticks) butter or margarine, softened
1 cup confectioners' sugar
2¼ cups unsifted all-purpose flour
½ teaspoon salt
½ teaspoon ground cardamom
2 large eggs
1 tablespoon water
Sugar cubes or rock candy

1. In large bowl, with electric mixer, beat butter and sugar until fluffy. With mixer on low speed, beat in flour, salt, cardamom, and 1 egg until well blended, occasionally scraping bowl with rubber spatula.
2. Heat oven to 350°F. Grease 2 baking sheets. In cup with fork, beat remaining egg with water. Place sugar cubes or rock candy in plastic bag; with rolling pin, crush to bits.
3. Using a measuring tablespoon, divide dough into 40 pieces. Roll each, one at a time, into 10-inch-long rope; shape rope to resemble a pretzel. Using wide metal spatula or

pancake turner, lift pretzels and place, 1-inch apart, on greased baking sheet. Brush pretzels with egg mixture. Sprinkle sugar on top.
4. Bake cookies 10 minutes or until golden. Cool cookies on wire racks. Store in airtight containers.

PISTACHIO-ALMOND LOGS

Photograph, opposite

The subtle flavors of almonds and pistachios play off each other in these pastry-based logs.

MAKES 3 DOZEN
1 11-ounce package piecrust mix or pastry for 2-crust pie
½ cup ground almonds
½ cup confectioners' sugar
2 large egg yolks
1 teaspoon almond extract
2 large egg whites
1½ cups finely chopped shelled unsalted pistachio nuts
¼ cup granulated sugar

1. Combine piecrust mix, almonds, and confectioners' sugar in bowl. Add egg yolks and extract; toss with fork until well mixed. Gather mixture into ball. If mixture is too dry to cling together, add water, a teaspoon at a time.
2. Knead dough a few times on a lightly floured surface until smooth. Heat oven to 400°F.
3. Divide dough into 12 pieces. Shape each piece into 12-inch-long roll. Cut each roll into thirds crosswise. Beat egg whites until foamy in shallow dish. Combine pistachio nuts and sugar in another shallow dish. Dip logs into whites; coat with sugared nuts. Place 1 inch apart on greased baking sheet. Bake until golden—about 12 minutes. Transfer to wire racks with broad spatula; cool.

DESSERTS

APPLE TART

Photograph, opposite

Sugar caramelizes to a shiny coating on this tasty, old-fashioned apple tart adapted from a 19th-century recipe.

MAKES 6 SERVINGS
1 unbaked 10-inch pie shell
2 large (1 pound) Granny Smith apples
1 teaspoon lemon juice
1 tablespoon butter
2 tablespoons sugar
⅛ teaspoon ground cinnamon

1. Heat oven to 425°F. Peel and slice apples. In bowl, toss apples with lemon juice. In large skillet, melt butter over medium heat; add apples and saute until tender crisp —about 4 minutes.
2. To assemble tart, using fork, arrange apple slices in concentric rings on pastry round. Combine sugar and cinnamon and sprinkle over apples.
3. Bake tart on top rack of oven 20 to 25 minutes or until golden and apples are tender. Remove to wire rack to cool. To serve, cut into 6 wedges.

APRICOT MINCEMEAT TARTS

Brandied apricots add a new twist to the traditional mincemeat tarts of the holiday season.

MAKES 8 TARTS
⅓ cup dried apricot halves
¾ cup brandy or apricot liqueur
1 11-ounce package piecrust mix
2 cups prepared mincemeat or 1 20-ounce jar mincemeat

1. At least 4 hours before preparing tarts, cut each apricot half into quarters. In small bowl, combine apricots and ½ cup brandy. Let stand, covered, 4 hours.
2. Heat oven to 425°F. Prepare piecrust mix following package directions. Divide into 8 balls. Roll each ball into 5-inch circle and fit into 3-inch-wide, 1½-inch-deep tart pan. Prick with fork. Bake 5 to 7 minutes or until golden brown. Let cool; remove tart pans and place shells on flameproof serving tray.
3. Just before serving, in 2-quart saucepan, combine mincemeat and apricot mixture. Heat to boiling, then spoon into tart shells.
4. Bring tarts to serving cart or side table. In long-handled ladle, gently warm remaining brandy until vapors rise. Ignite and pour over tops of tarts. When flames subside, serve.

DRIED-CHERRY PIE

Photograph, opposite

In early America, dried fruit made it possible to have pies long after fresh fruit was out of season. A dried-cherry pie was a special treat at holiday time.

MAKES 6 SERVINGS
1 unbaked 10-inch pie shell
¾ pound dried Michigan sour cherries (see note)
1½ cups water
5 teaspoons cornstarch
3 tablespoons sugar
1 teaspoon almond-flavored liqueur
2 teaspoons butter

1. Heat oven to 425°F. Crimp edge of pastry with tines of fork. Line pastry with aluminum foil; fill with pie weights or uncooked beans. Bake pastry for 15 minutes; remove weights and foil and bake pastry shell 5 minutes longer. Cool on wire rack.
2. In 2-quart saucepan, combine cherries and 1 cup water. Cook over low heat 10 minutes. In small bowl, beat together remaining water and cornstarch. Increase heat to medium, stir cornstarch mixture and sugar into cherry mixture. Cook, stirring, until cherry mixture boils and thickens. Cook 1 minute longer.
3. Remove cherry filling from heat. Stir in liqueur and butter until well combined. Pour into pastry shell. Cool to room temperature on wire rack. To serve, cut into 6 wedges.
Note: Dried cherries are available by mail order from American Spoon Foods, 411 E. Lake St., Petoskey, MI 49770, or by calling 1 (800) 222-5886.

Pretzels, recipe page 136; Apple Tart, recipe this page; Dried-Cherry Pie, recipe this page; Pound Cake, recipe page 153; on the tree, Edible Cookies to Hang, recipe page 101

It's a good idea to be on the lookout for kitchen gifts whenever browsing in antiques stores and culinary shops. An old bean pot picked up at a flea market becomes a homey gift when filled with packages of assorted dried beans and a couple of favorite bean recipes. The same goes for vintage blue jars with zinc lids; I will fill them with anything from popcorn to candy to potpourri. Friends always welcome holiday goodies when proffered in a piece of pottery or china that matches a collection. And a basket needs only a bow to become a handy present.

ALMOND FRUITCAKES

Beaten egg whites and sifted cake flour lighten these traditionally dense fruitcakes.

MAKES 3 SMALL LOAVES
1 12-ounce package diced mixed
    dried fruit
½ cup light rum or dry sherry
2 cups sifted cake flour
¾ cup cugar
1 teaspoon baking powder
¼ teaspoon salt
1 cup slivered blanched almonds,
    toasted
½ cup (1 stick) butter or margarine,
    melted
1 teaspoon vanilla extract
6 large egg whites (about ¾ cup), at
    room temperature
Whole blanched almonds
Light corn syrup for glazing or
    additional rum or sherry for
    soaking (optional)

1. In small bowl, combine dried fruit with rum or sherry; let soak 1 hour. Meanwhile, grease and flour three 5¾- by 3¼-inch loaf pans.
2. Heat oven to 325°F. In large bowl, combine flour, ½ cup sugar, baking powder, and salt. Add soaked-fruit mixture; stir until fruit is coated with flour mixture. Stir in slivered almonds, butter, and vanilla.
3. In small bowl, with electric mixer at high speed, beat egg whites until foamy. Gradually beat in remaining ¼ cup sugar until stiff peaks form. Fold in beaten egg whites, one third at a time, in prepared pans. Arrange or insert whole almonds on top.
4. Bake fruitcakes 1 hour or until toothpick inserted in center comes out clean. Cool in pans 10 minutes. Remove cakes from pans to wire racks; cool completely. For a shiny

glaze, heat corn syrup to boiling; brush on cakes and let dry. Wrap and store overnight before slicing.
5. If desired, cover cooled cakes completely in rum- or sherry-soaked cheesecloth. Wrap in aluminum foil and store in cool place. Resoak cheesecloth weekly until ready for gift-giving or serving. For gifts, wrap fruitcakes in plastic wrap.

COLONIAL APPLE PIE

The hands-down, all-American dessert, of Christmas and really every season, is apple pie. This interpretation of the historic recipe brings elegance and sophistication to the old favorite.

MAKES ONE 9-INCH FLAT PIE
1½ cups unsifted all-purpose flour
2 tablespoons sugar
½ cup (1 stick) butter or margarine
2 large eggs
Cold water
½ cup sugar
1 teaspoon ground cinnamon
Vanilla wafers (cookies)
7 Golden Delicious or green cooking
    apples
½ cup dried currants
2 tablespoons apple jelly

1. In a medium-size bowl, combine flour and 2 tablespoons sugar. With pastry blender, cut in butter until mixture resembles coarse crumbs. Beat eggs in a small measuring cup. Add enough cold water to measure ⅔ cup. Add about 5 tablespoons egg mixture to flour mixture while mixing lightly with a fork until pastry is moist enough to hold together. Gather pastry into a ball. (Reserve extra egg mixture.)
2. On lightly floured surface with floured rolling pin, roll pastry into a 14-inch circle. Carefully lift onto a large baking sheet. Chill pastry while preparing apples.

3. In small bowl, combine ½ cup sugar and cinnamon. Crush enough wafers to get ½ cup crumbs. Peel five of the apples; halve and remove cores with a melon ball cutter or quarter apples and cut out cores. Thinly slice the five apples.
4. Heat oven to 400°F. Remove pastry from refrigerator. Fold pastry ½ inch toward center along edge to form a double-thick edge. Brush pastry with some of the egg mixture. Sprinkle center of pastry with half the wafer crumbs to form a 9-inch circle. Arrange half of the apple slices in an even layer over crumbs. Sprinkle with half of the cinnamon sugar and currants.
5. Arrange remaining apple slices on top to form a neat, compact, even mound of apples about 9 inches in diameter and 2 inches high. It should look like a cake pan sitting in the middle of the pastry. Sprinkle apples with remaining crumbs, cinnamon sugar, and currants. If desired, reserve 1 tablespoon currants to sprinkle over top layer of apples.
6. Peel, core, and cut remaining 2 apples into thin slices. Arrange on top in an attractive pattern around edge and in the center. Bring the pastry all around up and over the mound of apples to form an open "bag." The pastry will naturally form gathers or pleats; press pastry firmly on top to secure to top edge of apples and keep pastry from opening during baking. Brush outer pastry edge with egg mixture. Cover center of pie with circle of aluminum foil.
7. Bake pie 25 minutes. Lower oven temperature to 350°F. Continue to bake until juices bubble and apples are tender—about 20 minutes. If pastry over browns, cover with strips of aluminum foil. Remove foil from center 5 minutes before done.
8. Cool pie completely. Melt apple jelly in a small saucepan. Brush over apple slices and pastry on top.

FRUITCAKE CUPS

These individual fruitcakes are chock-full of candied fruits and nuts, and lightly spiced with cinnamon and nutmeg.

MAKES ABOUT 2½ DOZEN
½ cup (1 stick) butter or margarine
1 cup sugar
1 cup water
½ cup brandy
1 cup dark seedless raisins
1 8-ounce package chopped pitted dates
3 cups unsifted all-purpose flour
1 teaspoon baking soda
1 teaspoon ground cinnamon
¾ teaspoon salt
½ teaspoon ground nutmeg
2 large eggs
2 8-ounce packages chopped candied mixed fruit
1 cup chopped pecans
Whole candied red cherries
Candied green cherries, quartered

1. Grease and flour thirty 2½-inch muffin-pan cups or line with foil-and-paper muffin-cup liners.
2. In 2-quart saucepan, combine butter, sugar, water, brandy, raisins, and dates. Heat to boiling over high heat. Reduce heat to low; cook 10 minutes, stirring occasionally. Remove from heat and set aside to cool completely.
3. In large bowl, combine 2 cups flour, the soda, cinnamon, salt, and nutmeg. Stir in cooled date mixture. Add eggs and stir until well mixed.
4. Heat oven to 275°F. In medium-size bowl or plastic bag, toss candied fruit and pecans with remaining 1 cup flour until well coated. Add to batter, stirring to mix well. Spoon batter into prepared muffin cups, filling each two-thirds full. Place a whole red cherry in center of each with quartered green cherries on each side.

5. Bake fruitcakes 1 hour and 10 minutes, or until cake tester inserted in center comes out clean. Remove cakes to wire racks to cool completely. Store in airtight container.

POUND CAKE

Photograph, page 148

This pound cake was adapted from a recipe that appeared in the 1794-1817 account book of Lebanon County, Pa., furnituremaker Peter Ranck.

MAKES 16 SERVINGS
1½ cups butter
2¼ cups sugar
6 eggs
¾ cup milk
2 teaspoons vanilla
3 cups flour
½ teaspoon baking soda
½ teaspoon salt
Glaze (recipe follows)

1. Cream butter and sugar. Add eggs, one at a time. Mix vanilla with milk and add alternately to creamed mixture with sifted flour, soda, and salt.
2. Turn batter into a greased and floured tube pan. Bake at 250°F for about one hour and 20 minutes. Remove from oven and let cool 15 minutes. Turn out onto cake rack and let cool completely.

GLAZE

1 cup confectioners' sugar
2 tablespoons vegetable shortening
3 to 4 teaspoons water
Chopped nuts (optional)

In small bowl, with electric mixer, beat together sugar, vegetable shortening and water until smooth. Spread glaze over top of cake, allowing some to run down side. Sprinkle with chopped nuts, if desired.

EGGNOG CAKES

Photograph, page 132

Convenient cake mix is the basis of this unusual dessert topped with nuts.

MAKES 12 SMALL OR
1 LARGE BUNDT CAKE
½ cup finely chopped walnuts or pecans
1 18¼-ounce package yellow cake mix
1 cup refrigerated or canned eggnog
¼ cup vegetable oil
3 large eggs
2 tablespoons rum or orange juice
¼ teaspoon ground nutmeg

1. Generously grease and flour 12 individual-size (1 cup) Bundt pans (see Note) or a 10-inch (12-cup) Bundt pan. Sprinkle nuts in bottom of prepared pans (about 2 teaspoons in each individual pan); set aside.
2. Heat oven to 350°F for indivdual-size pans or 325°F for 10-inch pan.
3. In large bowl, with electric mixer at low speed, combine dry cake mix, eggnog, oil, eggs, rum, and nutmeg; beat 2 minutes. Pour batter into prepared pans, filling each individual pan half full.
4. Bake individual cakes 20 to 25 minutes or 10-inch cake 1 hour, or until cake tester inserted in center comes out clean. Cool in pan on wire rack 15 minutes. Remove cakes from pans to wire rack to cool completely. Store cakes in airtight container.
Note: If baking individual cakes in batches, be sure to wipe pan clean with paper towels and generously grease and flour before reusing. Individual-size Bundt pans (6 to a pan) are available by mail from Maid of Scandinavia, 3244 Raleigh Ave., Minneapolis, MN, 55416. Or, call 1 (800) 328-6722.

PLUM PUDDING WITH HARD SAUCE

This is an updated version of Tiny Tim's favorite Christmas pudding.

MAKES 10 TO 12 SERVINGS

1 cup all-purpose flour
½ teaspoon salt
1½ teaspoons ground cinnamon
½ teaspoon ground nutmeg
½ teaspoon ground allspice
½ teaspoon ground mace
1 cup dried bread crumbs
¾ cup butter or margarine
1 cup firmly packed light-
   brown sugar
4 large eggs
3 cups chopped mixed candied fruit
1½ cups raisins
¾ cups slivered blanched almonds
½ cup brandy
Holly leaves and fresh cranberries
   for garnish
Hard Sauce (recipe follows)

1. Heavily grease a 2½-quart steamed pudding mold with lid, or metal mixing bowl. If using a bowl, cut piece of foil 1 inch larger than top of bowl to use as lid; set aside. Dust inside of mold with sugar, tapping out any excess.
2. In a small bowl, combine first 8 ingredients.
3. In large bowl with electric mixer at medium speed, beat butter with sugar until fluffy. Beat in eggs one at a time. At low speed, beat in flour mixture until well mixed. Fold in candied fruit, raisins, and almonds. Spoon into prepared mold; cover with lid. If using mixing bowl, cover bowl with foil; tie tightly with string.
4. Set mold on trivet in 8-quart saucepot. Pour enough boiling water into the saucepot to surround

Plum Pudding with Hard Sauce, recipe this page

the lower half of the mold. Over high heat, heat to boiling. Reduce heat to low; cover and simmer 3 hours or until skewer inserted comes out clean. (Keep water boiling gently during cooking time, adding more water, if needed.)
5. Cool pudding in mold 10 minutes. Loosen around edge with knife; invert onto plate. In a small saucepan, heat brandy to lukewarm. Top pudding with holly; stud pudding with cranberries, inserting half a toothpick into each cranberry, inserting other end of toothpick into pudding. Pour warm brandy around side of pudding and ignite. Serve with Hard Sauce.

HARD SAUCE

⅓ cup butter, softened
1¼ cups confectioners' sugar
1 teaspoon vanilla

In small bowl with electric mixer at medium speed, beat butter with 1 cup confectioners' sugar and vanilla until creamy. Beat in the remaining ¼ cup confectioners' sugar until fluffy, if needed.

PUMPKIN MOUSSE

Mousse is a French dessert most often associated with flavors such as chocolate or raspberry, a dish made light and airy with whipped cream and egg whites. Our interpretation relies on native pumpkin for a more beguiling play of texture and flavor.

MAKES 16 SERVINGS
1 cup milk
2 envelopes unflavored gelatin
*1 20-ounce can solid-packed
    pumpkin*
1½ teaspoons ground cinnamon
1 teaspoon ground ginger
1 teaspoon ground nutmeg
¾ teaspoon salt
¼ teaspoon ground cloves
6 eggs, separated
1 cup sugar
2 cups heavy or whipping cream
¼ cup finely chopped walnuts

1. In heavy 3-quart saucepan, mix milk and gelatin; let stand 1 minute. Cook over medium heat until gelatin is completely dissolved, stirring constantly. Stir in pumpkin, cinnamon, ginger, nutmeg, salt, cloves, egg yolks, and ¾ cup sugar. Cook over medium-low heat until mixture is very thick, about 10 minutes, stirring contantly (do not boil or mix-

ture will curdle). Refrigerate until mixture is well chilled, but not set, about 4½ hours, stirring occasionally. (If pumpkin mixture is not well chilled, the cream will curdle when folded in.)
2. Meanwhile, prepare collar for 1½-quart soufflé dish: From roll of waxed paper, tear off a 24-inch strip; fold in half lengthwise. Wrap waxed paper around outside of dish so collar stands 3 inches above rim. Secure with cellophane tape.
3. When pumpkin mixture is chilled, in large bowl with mixer at high speed, beat egg whites until soft peaks form. Beating at high speed, gradually sprinkle in ¼ cup sugar, beating until sugar is dissolved. (Whites should stand in stiff, glossy peaks.)
4. In small bowl with mixer at medium speed beat 1½ cups cream.
5. With wire whisk or rubber spatula, gently fold whipped cream and pumpkin mixture into beaten egg whites. Spoon mixture into soufflé dish; refrigerate until set—about 2 hours.
6. In small bowl with mixer at medium speed, beat remaining heavy cream until stiff peaks form. Garnish mousse with whipped cream and chopped walnuts.

GINGER CUSTARD

Photograph, below

"Pour" custard or "boiled" custard was a favorite dish in colonial times, flavored with vanilla or brandy and served in a glass or dessert dish, or poured over cake.

MAKES 6 SERVINGS
3 cups milk
4 eggs
¼ cup sugar
⅛ teaspoon salt
*2 tablespoons syrup from preserved
    ginger*
¼ cup chopped preserved ginger
Cinnamon (optional)
Sliced preserved ginger (optional)

1. In a medium-sized heavy saucepan, heat 2½ cups of milk until bubbles form around edges.
2. Beat eggs and remaining milk together until frothy. Stir egg mixture into hot milk, along with sugar and salt; continue heating, stirring constantly, until mixture thickens and coats a metal spoon.
3. Remove custard from heat; stir in syrup and chopped ginger. Pour into serving bowl and chill completely. If desired, garnish with cinnamon and sliced ginger just before serving.

Ginger Custard, recipe this page

SNOW EGGS
(Oeufs à la Neige)
Photograph, opposite

Beloved by all, this simple and versatile old-fashioned French dessert is served in the nursery and at formal dinner parties.

MAKES 6 TO 8 SERVINGS
3 cups milk
1 vanilla bean
6 large egg yolks
1 cup sugar
1 teaspoon brandy or kirsch
Pinch of salt
3 large egg whites, at room
*   temperature*
Caramel Syrup (optional; recipe
*   follows)*

1. In nonaluminum, 2-quart saucepan, heat milk and vanilla bean over a low heat 10 minutes. Remove vanilla bean; wash and dry to use again, if desired.
2. In 4-cup measuring cup used for milk, or in a small bowl, beat egg yolks, ½ cup sugar, the brandy, and salt. Beat in a little warm milk. Beat yolk mixture back into milk in saucepan. Heat gently over low heat, stirring constantly, until mixture thickens slightly and coats a spoon—about 15 minutes. Pour custard into large shallow serving dish and set aside to cool.
3. Fill large skillet halfway with water and heat to simmering. In small bowl, beat egg whites until foamy. Gradually add remaining ½ cup sugar, beating until stiff peaks form. With large spoon, scoop up egg-white meringue and shape into a large oval or "egg" with the help of another spoon or spatula. Slide meringue "egg" into simmering water. Poach "eggs" 6 at a time, for 3 minutes. Gently turn "eggs" and poach 3 minutes longer. Remove with slotted spoon to drain on paper towels.

4. Arrange "eggs" on top of cooled custard in serving dish. Refrigerate until serving time.
5. Before serving, prepare Caramel Syrup. Drizzle over meringue "eggs."

CARAMEL SYRUP
½ cup sugar
1 tablespoon water

In small saucepan, combine sugar and water until well mixed. Cook over low heat until sugar is completely dissolved and amber in color. Do not stir the sugar as it melts but swirl the pan so it melts evenly. Cool a few minutes before using.

YULE LOG
(Bûche aux Marrons)
Photograph, opposite

To serve this scrumptious chocolate-chestnut recipe, cut the log into thin slices with a knife dipped in very hot water.

MAKES 12 SERVINGS
1 8-ounce package semisweet
*   chocolate squares, coarsely*
*   chopped*
1 15½-ounce can chestnut purée
*   (see note)*
¾ cup confectioners' sugar
½ cup (1 stick) unsalted butter,
*   softened*
½ cup finely chopped, blanched,
*   sliced almonds*
Candied violets or roses and green
*   leaves for garnish (optional)*

1. In top of double boiler, melt chocolate over hot, not boiling, water. With hand-held electric mixer, beat chestnut purée, confectioners' sugar, and butter into chocolate. Or, combine ingredients in a food processor. Beat or stir in almonds. Refrigerate 4 to 5 hours.
2. Scoop chilled chocolate-chestnut mixture onto work surface. Set aside ¼ cup. With wet, warm hands, shape remainder into 8-inch-long log, dipping hands into bowl of warm water when they get sticky. Place log on doily-lined serving plate. Shape reserved mixture into 2 "knots" and mold one onto side and other on top of log.
3. In 1-quart saucepan, heat 3 inches water to boiling. Dip a fork into boiling water and make striations along the log to resemble bark. Refrigerate until ready to serve. Garnish with candied violets and green leaves, if desired.
Note: This candy is equally good when made with almond paste, if chestnut purée is not available. Use 13 ounces or about 1½ cups almond paste and reduce sugar to ½ cup.

Yule Log, recipe this page, and *Snow Eggs,* recipe this page

BEVERAGES

GOLDEN WASSAIL WITH HOT BUTTERED APPLES

Photograph, opposite

Old wassail recipes are exotic concoctions of baked apples, spiced ale, Madeira or sherry, and, sometimes, brandy, mixed with stiffly beaten egg whites and yolks. The key ingredient, however, was the repeated Saxon toast "Wass hael," or "Be well." We have included the baked apples to lend a buttery flavor to our lightly alcoholic spiced cider punch.

MAKES ABOUT 20 SERVINGS
1 gallon filtered cider
4 cinnamon sticks, each about 3 inches long
1 tablespoon whole cloves
1 whole nutmeg or 1 teaspoon whole allspice
¼ cup lemon juice
½ cup orange juice
1 large lemon, sliced
1 large orange, sliced
4 cups applejack
¼ cup light brown sugar (optional)
Baked Lady Apples (recipe follows)

1. Mix cider, cinnamon, cloves, nutmeg, juices, and fruit slices in a large pot.
2. Bring just to boiling over high heat. Lower heat and simmer 20 minutes.
3. Add applejack and heat mixture 3 minutes more. Taste and add sugar, 1 tablespoon at time, as desired, to round off flavor.

4. Pour into heated punch bowl (or leave in the pot) and gently ease the apples in to float on top.
Note: If you feel some guests might enjoy a slightly more alcoholic beverage, set out a small pitcher of heated dark rum and add about 1 tablespoon to each serving. Another nice touch is a bowl of lightly sweetened whipped cream and a shaker of nutmeg to turn the punch into Hot Apple Chantilly.

BAKED LADY APPLES

Lady apples are the tiny golden ones with a pink blush and can be seen around Christmastime in many areas. If you can't find them, substitute other small apples, not more than 4 ounces each.

8 lady apples or other small apples
Whole cloves
4 teaspoons butter or margarine
Water

1. Heat oven to 350°F. Press several cloves into each apple.
2. Place apples in a baking dish with about ⅛ inch water. Dot with butter. Bake about 20 minutes until tender but not mushy.

CAFÉ BRÛLOT

This strong, zesty coffee recipe is traditionally made and served in a chafing dish; it may also be prepared in a skillet and transferred to a small punch bowl.

MAKES 8 SERVINGS
Zest or peel of 1 orange
Zest or peel of 1 lemon
1 short cinnamon stick
6 whole cloves
4 teaspoons sugar
¾ cup cognac or armagnac, warmed
1 quart strong hot coffee

1. In chafing dish, combine orange and lemon peels, cinnamon stick, cloves, sugar, and cognac. Use a long match to ignite cognac. Stir to dissolve sugar.
2. Slowly add coffee; stir well. Serve in demitasse cups.

MULLED CIDER

Colonial taverns were ready at a moment's notice to serve up a steaming mug of mulled cider to a weary traveler. Cider mugs were filled from a barrel (occasionally spices were added), while mulling irons, heated to a glowing red in the fireplace, were plunged into each mug, instantly warming the cider.

MAKES 8 SERVINGS
1 half-gallon natural apple cider
1 tablespoon whole allspice
1 tablespoon whole cloves
8 long cinnamon sticks

In 3-quart saucepan, heat cider, allspice, cloves, and cinnamon sticks to boiling. If not using mulling irons, place cinnamon stick into each of 8 mugs. Strain hot cider into mugs and serve.

Golden Wassail with Hot Buttered Apples, recipe this page

FLAMING BOURBON PUNCH

This is a spirited punch with a spicy fragrance. Its dramatic flaming presentation makes it a good choice for a Christmas Night party.

MAKES 4 QUARTS
3 quarts apple cider
¼ cup lemon juice
¼ cup firmly packed light-brown sugar
1 tablespoon whole cloves
3 3-inch cinnamon sticks
1 teaspoon whole allspice
1 red apple, unpeeled and thinly sliced
3½ cups bourbon

Spicy Wine Punch, recipe this page

1. In 6-quart kettle, combine cider, lemon juice, brown sugar, cloves, cinnamon, and allspice. Heat just to boiling. Leave the punch in kettle or carefully pour into flameproof punch bowl on serving cart or side table. Stir in apple slices and 3 cups bourbon.
2. In long-handled ladle, gently warm remaining bourbon until vapors rise. Ignite and pour over punch. When flames subside, ladle into heatproof glasses, punch cups, or mugs.

CAPPUCCINO NOG

This frothy coffee-milk drink is a delicious variation of classic eggnog. In place of rum, its coffee flavor is intensified by adding a coffee liqueur.

MAKES 12 ONE-CUP SERVINGS
12 large eggs
⅓ cup sugar
6 cups milk
3 cups Kahlúa, Tia Maria, or other coffee liqueur
½ teaspoon ground nutmeg
½ cup heavy cream
Additional ground nutmeg for garnish (optional)

1. In large bowl, with electric mixer at medium speed, beat eggs until foamy. Gradually add sugar and beat until thick and lemon-colored—5 minutes.
2. Reduce mixer speed to low; gradually add milk, liqueur, and nutmeg. Cover and refrigerate until well chilled.
3. Before serving, in medium-size bowl, beat cream until stiff peaks form. With wire whisk, gently fold whipped cream into chilled egg mixture. Pour into punch bowl and sprinkle top with additional nutmeg, if desired.

SPICY WINE PUNCH

Photograph, left

Fragrant and fruity, this warm punch should be served in mugs.

MAKES 32 ONE-CUP SERVINGS
3 1.5-liter bottles dry red wine
3 cups dark seedless raisins
2 cups sugar
1½ cups chopped dried figs
3 3-inch cinnamon sticks
3 ½-inch-thick slices fresh gingerroot
2 cups brandy
Clove-Studded Orange Slices (recipe follows)

1. In nonaluminum 10-quart saucepan, combine wine, raisins, sugar, figs, cinnamon sticks, and gingerroot. Heat to simmering over medium-low heat, stirring until sugar dissolves. Simmer 5 minutes.
2. Remove wine mixture from heat; let stand 5 minutes. Remove and discard cinnamon sticks and gingerroot. Add brandy and pour mixture into heatproof serving bowl. Garnish with studded orange slices, if desired.

CLOVE-STUDDED ORANGE SLICES

Cut 1 navel orange crosswise into ¼-inch-thick slices. Discard end slices. Stud the rind of each slice with whole cloves.

SPARKLING CHRISTMAS PUNCH

Cranberry juice and vodka are simmered with spices, then chilled and sparkled with soda.

MAKES 40 ONE-CUP SERVINGS
2 3-inch cinnamon sticks, crushed
1 teaspoon whole allspice
1 5-inch-square piece cheesecloth
String or twine
3 quarts apple cider
3 quarts cranberry juice cocktail
Juice of 3 oranges, strained
⅓ cup firmly packed brown sugar
3 1-liter bottles club soda or seltzer, chilled
6 cups vodka, chilled
Apple-Cranberry Garnishes (optional; recipe follows)

1. Place cinnamon and allspice on cheesecloth. Pull up edges of cloth and tie into bag with string or twine.
2. In nonaluminum, 8-quart saucepot, combine cider, cranberry juice, orange juice, and brown sugar. Heat to simmering over medium-low heat. Add spice bag and simmer 20 minutes. Remove from heat; cover and cool to room temperature. Refrigerate overnight.
3. Before serving, remove spice bag. Pour punch into serving bowl. Stir in club soda and vodka. Garnish with cut-out apple slices, if desired. Serve punch in mugs garnished with skewered apple stars and cranberries, if desired.

Sparkling Christmas Punch, recipe this page

APPLE-CRANBERRY GARNISHES

To make, cut ¼-inch slices from top to bottom of large green apples. Toss slices with lemon juice. With small star-shaped or other holiday cookie cutter, cut out center of each apple slice. Reserve the cut-out shapes to skewer with cranberries. Float apple slices on punch. To make the garnishes for mugs, on wooden skewers, thread a cranberry, then the apple cut-out shape, then another cranberry.

CREAMY ALL-AMERICAN EGGNOG

Rich with the goodness of fresh eggs, heavy cream, and milk, eggnog is truly nourishing; rich with bourbon or Tennessee whiskey, it's truly tippling.

MAKES ABOUT 24 SERVINGS
1 dozen large eggs
1½ cups sugar
1 liter bourbon or Tennessee whiskey
1 quart heavy cream
1 quart milk
Whipped cream (optional)
Ground nutmeg (optional)
Cinnamon sticks (optional)

1. Separate eggs. In large bowl with mixer at low speed, beat egg yolks and 1 cup sugar until blended. At high speed, beat until thick and lemon-colored. Gradually beat in bourbon. Refrigerate until cold.
2. In punch bowl, combine egg yolk mixture, cream, and milk. In large bowl with mixer at high speed, beat egg whites until soft peaks form. Gradually beat in remaining ½ cup sugar until stiff peaks form. With wire whisk, stir egg whites into yolk mixture until mixed. Top with whipped cream and a sprinkle of nutmeg; serve with cinnamon sticks, if desired.

CHAPTER SIX

THE CHRISTMAS WORKSHOP

RESOURCE DIRECTORY

RESOURCE DIRECTORY

The following is a reference guide to some of the wonderful Christmas accessories, handicrafts, and collectibles featured on the pages of *Country Christmas*. Many of the products are handcrafted originals, while others are sold as kits, to assemble at home. We're also including a few of our favorite, exotic foods available by mail order.

Anchor Hocking
2980 West Fair Ave.
Lancaster, OH 43132
(614) 687-2111

Glass tableware.

The Art Institute of Chicago
Michigan Ave. at Adams St.
Chicago, IL 60603
1 (800) 624-9000

Mugs, posters, ornaments, etc.

Arts Americana
P.O. Box 329
Tilghman Island, MD 21671

Handcrafted wood figurines.

As Good As Old
5933 McCallum St.
Philadelphia, PA 19144
1 (800) 331-2408

Calendars, wreaths, shelves, mirrors, painted by hand.

Laura Ashley, Inc.
714 Madison Ave.
New York, NY 10021
(212) 735-5000

Kitchen and bathroom gift ideas.

Blanchard & Blanchard Ltd.
P.O. Box 1080
Norwich, VT 05055
1 (800) 334-0286

*Salad dressings, ketchup,
mustards, and dessert sauces.*

**The Brightine Monks
Gourmet Confections**
23300 Walker Ln.
Amity, OR
(503) 835-8080

*Price list. Rich fudge produced
daily; truffles and almond bark.*

**Cadwell Furniture and
Accessories**
P.O. Box 1155
Toccoa, GA 30577
(404) 886-5598

*Rocking chairs, collectibles,
baskets, shelves, etc.*

Candlertown Chairworks
P.O. Box 1630C
Candler, NC 28715
(704) 667-4844

*Catalogue $2. Wooden chairs,
stools, etc.*

Celebrations
5436 Naples Drive
Huber Heights, OH 45424
(513) 236-8759

*Beeswax candles, ornaments in
various shapes.*

C'est Croissant, Inc.
22138 So. Vermont Ave., Suite F
Torrence, CA 90502
1 (800) 633-2767

*Brochure. Croissant and
preserves packages.*

The Charleston Cake Lady
P.O. Box 30683
Charleston, SC 29417
(803) 766-7173

*Price list. Poppyseed, Macaroon,
Banana Pineapple and other
cakes.*

Mary Kay Colling
566 Pinegrove Ave.
Rochester, NY 14617

*Stencilled notecards and
envelopes.*

Cookie of the Month
Box 155
Koalin Rd.
Avondale, PA 19311

*Brochure. Cookies of the month
packages.*

Country Wood Products, Inc.
510 Second Ave.
Wayland, NY 14572
(716) 728-5745

*Wall and table carved wood
decorations.*

Crabtree & Evelyn
P.O. Box 167
Woodstock, CT 06281
1 (800) 624-5211

*Brochure. Tins and baskets of
sweets and biscuits perfect for
teatime.*

**Katha Diddel Home
Collection**
420 Madison Ave.
Suite 806
New York, NY 10017
1 (800) 289-8946

*Ornaments, stockings, baby
linens.*

Gooseberry Patch
P.O. Box 634
Delaware, OH 43015
(614) 369-1554

*Catalog. Cookie cutters,
ornaments, tree skirts, etc.*

June Grigg Designs, Inc.
3427 Oakcliff Rd.
Suite 112
Atlanta, GA 30340
(404) 452-8075

*Brochure. P. Buckley Moss
counted-cross-stitch needlework
designs; samplers, miniatures,
etc.*

Tracey Jamar
250 Riverside Dr.
New York, NY 10025
(212) 866-6426

Handmade tree ornaments.

Jamison Farm
171 Jamison Ln.
Latrobe, PA 15650
1 (800) 237-LAMB

*Brochure. Hormone- and
antibiotics-free lamb.*

Krön Chocolatier, Inc.
120 Park Ave.
New York, NY 10017
1 (800) 370-5355

*Brochure. Chocolate assortments
and fancifully shaped novelties.*

Kron Enterprises
P.O. Box 348
Canastota, NY 13032-0348
1 (800) 447-6011

*Lighting fixtures, stars, wooden
ornaments.*

B. Lease & Sons, Inc.
23 E. Depot St.
Lichtfield, MN 55355
(612) 693-7868

Wooden carved deer, animals, etc.

Mabel's
849 Madison Ave.
New York, NY 10021
(212) 734-3263

Brochure. Original works of art.

**Midwest Importers of
Cannon Falls, Inc.**
P.O. Box 20, Hwy. 52 South
Cannon Falls, MN 55009
1 (800) 776-1020

*Catalog. Nutcrackers, music
boxes, wooden figures.*

**Museum of American Folk Art
Book & Gift Shop**
2 Lincoln Sq.
New York, NY 10023

*Various handcrafted gifts from
American craftspeople.*

**Ted and Rebecca Nichol's
Noah's Ark**
2909 Old Ocean City Rd.
Salisbury, MD 21801
(301) 546-9522

*Woodcarvings, animals, figurines,
staffs.*

Papercraft Corp.
Papercraft Park
Pittsburgh, PA 15238
1 (800) 245-6352

Giftwrap, ribbons, trimmings, etc.

The Plaid Bear
P.O. Box 23498
Lexington, KY 40523

*Paper dolls, teddy bears and
stuffed toys.*

The Ram's Horn Connection
2824 W. Munroe St.
Bethel Park, PA 15102
(412) 854-2167

*Brochure $1. Wool lamb/sheep
ornaments.*

Rowhouse Press
P.O. Box 20531
New York, NY 10025

*Catalog $2.50. Prints, posters,
pattern kits, workbooks.*

Tree Toys
P.O. Box 492
Hinsdale, IL 60521
(708) 323-6505

*Tree ornaments, holiday
patterns, kits.*

**Upper Canada Coffee Works
& Tea Mill, Inc.**
612 Gordon Baker Rd.
Willowdale, Ontario
M2H 3B4 Canada
(416) 494-9700

*Price list. Congou tea pressed in-
to "bricks" to brew or display.*

Vaillancourt Folk Art
145 Armsby Rd.
Sutton, MA 01590
(508) 865-9183

*Chalkware-table pieces, molded
statues, etc.*

The Vermont Country Store
Mail-Order Office
P.O. Box 3000
Manchester, VT 05255-3000
(802) 362-2400

*Catalog. Clove, maple and
sassafras drops; other old-time
treats.*

Eldred Wheeler
3941 San Felipe
Houston, TX 77027
(713) 622-6225

*Redware, serving, and decorative
pieces.*

Sonya Whitaker
Route 1, Box 420
Mocksville, NC 27028
(704) 634-3794

*Brochure $2. Nativity sets,
wreaths, baskets, woodwork.*

Wicker By Design
2705 Newquay St.
Durham, NC 27705
(919) 383-6212

*Custom wicker furniture for
children.*

Wilderness Gourmet
P.O. Box 3257
Ann Arbor, MI 48106

*Price list. Venison steaks and
roasts, wild-boar hams, etc.*

Windsor Chairmaker
RR 2, Box 7
Lincolnville, ME 04849
(207) 789-5188

*Brochure. Windsor chairs, High
Boys, china cabinets, dining
tables, etc.*

We know we are very much alive when, head bowed against a blast of cold air, we hurry on our errands. It is a good feeling. On a clear, cold night, the sky is lit by the winter moon and a scattering of stars. Country life is captured forever in our memories in a photographic mix of shadows and shimmering light. In December, we are never too young or too old to store up memories of the pleasures around us.

INDEX

PHOTOGRAPHY CREDITS

Illustration Page 15, T. De Thulstrup, from *Harper's Weekly*, December 25, 1880

Snowflakes and snowbirds, the holly tree decked out in clusters of scarlet berries, cold wind whistling around the chimney cap, Canadian geese feeding in the field beyond the lane, fruitcake resting in a richness of brandy—soon it will be Christmas.

Acknowledgments

I t goes without saying, of course, that Christmas is a time of making special efforts for family and friends, but the many caring homeowners who opened their houses and decorated them specifically for *Country Living,* with grace and without complaint, certainly granted the magazine a dear gift that cannot in any way be measured, or adequately repaid. We want to thank each and every one from the bottom of our hearts.

We want, too, to thank and acknowledge the editors on the staff of *Country Living* who have, over the years, directed and styled photography of our Christmas houses and holiday food featured herein: Niña Williams, Peggy Drexler, Jane Makley, Nancy Mernit, Laura Lombardi, Anne Leonard Hardy, Jason Kontos, Robin Long Mayer and Doretta Sperduto; and thanks too, to Aña Castillo Erickson, who designed our homemade ornaments. The development of seasonal recipes and the food styling were capably and beautifully undertaken by Lucy Wing and Joanne Lamb Hayes and their dedicated staff.

Finally, for their tireless efforts in locating and culling slides from our archives, we wish to thank both Louise Fiore and Theo Hewko.